THE ECONOMICS OF NONPROFIT ENTERPRISE

A Study in Applied Economic Theory

Robert Scott Gassler

Guilford College

UNIVERSITY PRESS OF AMERICA

LANHAM • NEW YORK • LONDON

Copyright © 1986 by

University Press of America,® Inc.

4720 Boston Way
Lanham, MD 20706

3 Henrietta Street
London WC2E 8LU England

Library of Congress Cataloging in Publication Data

Gassler, Robert Scott.
    The economics of nonprofit enterprise.

    Bibliography: p.
    Includes index.
    1. Corporations, Nonprofit.   2. Neoclassical
school of economics.   I. Title.
HD62.6.G37   1986   338.7'4   85-26423
ISBN 0-8191-5148-8 (alk. paper)
ISBN 0-8191-5149-1 (pbk. : alk. paper)

m.R

to my parents,

Robert Karl Gassler and Lois Conard Gassler

iii

Acknowledgements

The largest debt I owe is to my adviser, Professor Kenneth Boulding, who encouraged me to choose the subject as a dissertation topic, inspired me to take as creative an approach as I could, and of course provided many helpful comments. Professor Judith A. Thornton of the University of Washington was the first person to encourage me in this direction, and she provided helpful comments later on. Professor Reuben Zubow's course on public finance formed the basis for Chapter II., especially the section on evaluation, and indirectly influenced the rest of the dissertation.

John Goulet of the Colby College Department of Mathematics verified the mathematics in Chapter IV. Robin Grace pointed out to me the concept of what I call "delineation of commodities."

Chapter I is based on an earlier paper [Gassler, 1979]. The Appendix to Chapter III was previously published in the Guilford Review, No. 18, Fall 1983, issue devoted to "Works in Progress."

Many persons provided encouragement and helpful comments along the way: Edward Ames, Abram Bergson, Elise Boulding, Carol A.M. Clark, Frank Columbo, Thomas Dernburg, Nancy DeWath, Pamela J. Doty, Richard Dye, Helene Ebenfield, Janos Horvath, Leonid Hurwicz, Richard Hydell, Karen Leppel, Fritz Machlup, Jay Marchand, James Meehan, Craig Smith, Tom Wildavsky, Robert G. Williams, and Wesley Yordon. Several helpful comments were received at seminars given at Colby College, Virginia Commonwealth University, the Colby-Bates-Bowdoin Economics Corsortium, and Wake Forest University. Richard Kendall and Lyman Randall provided two examples in Chapter III at Guilford College on "What Changes Are Needed in the U.S. Economy?" sponsored by the Friends Committee on National Legislation. The bulk of the original dissertation was written in 1978-1979 under a University Fellowship at the University of Colorado at Boulder.

I have tried not to leave anyone out deliberately, but for that and any other remaining errors, as well as all opinions, I take full responsibility.

Contents

Illustrations

ix

Preface

I first became interested in nonprofit organizations while studying the library industry. I had worked for a time in The New York Public Library, a fascinating blend of public and private nonprofit enterprise, and my dissertation was originally going to be on the economics of the library industry. Gradually, however, I found myself devoting more and more attention to the characteristics of private and public organizations, and the dissertation emerged with only a single chapter and an appendix on libraries.

One of the things that distracted me was the reaction I got when I told other economists that I was studying nonprofit organizations under Kenneth Boulding. Nearly everyone I talked with about the topic seemed eager to tell stories about how nonprofit organizations have distorted the original purposes for which they were designed, but no one seemed very clear on what those original purposes were. I decided that the reason for this was that economists were working with a neoclassical theory that is somehow too narrow for the scope of the problem, so the first draft of my dissertation was a ringing critique of the narrowness of the neoclassical paradigm. I got tired of that after a while; it seems that every graduate student goes through that stage. What I decided to do then was figure out just where the neoclassical failed and where it could be modified to fit into some larger framework that could serve more adequately.

I no longer feel as lonely as I did when I started; the study of nonprofit organizations is now a sizable and growing field. The <u>Journal of Economic Literature</u> has even given nonprofit industries their own classification number.

This book, a revision of my dissertation, is intended as a review of the literature on the economics of nonprofit enterprises and a contribution to its definition and direction. An overview of the chapters is provided in the introduction and a summary in the last chapter. Prerequisite for all but part of Chapter IV is a course in the principles of economics that includes minimal coverage of market failure. The mathematical model presented in Chapter IV can be read by anyone with a knowledge equivalent to Baumol (1977), Chapter 4; Nicholson (1978), Chapter 2; or Chiang (1967), Chapter 19.

CHAPTER I

INTRODUCTION

Purpose and Scope

Human social organization is as complex as human behavior, and the varieties of groups into which people can arrange themselves are probably too vast in number ever to be completely cataloged by anthropologists and sociologists. Indeed it is probably safe to say that (profit-making) firms have accounted for only a small fraction of the economic activity of human beings. Family and kinship systems, tribes, churches, governments, armies, universities, foundations, empires, and virtually all organizations in socialist countries have had a much larger hand in economic affairs than a superficial look at traditional neoclassical economics might suggest.

Recently, however, a number of economists have begun looking at many of these organizations using the tools of neoclassical theory to analyze them [e.g., Alchian, 1977; Baumol, 1973; Clarkson, 1980; Newhouse, 1970]. It is the contention here that such tools, at their present stage of development, are only partly suited for the task. The reason is that nonprofit enterprises perform functions in the economy which are far too broad in scope to fit neoclassical assumptions. In some cases nonprofit enterprises perform tasks which traditional neoclassical theory assumes to have been performed before market transactions take place; therefore the neoclassical model in such cases assumes away the problem to be solved.

To elaborate this central point we ask a series of questions: (1) What are nonprofit enterprises? (2) What do nonprofit enterprises do? (3) Why are nonprofit enterprises created? (4) How do nonprofit enterprises operate? (5) How efficiently do nonprofit enterprises perform? In discussing each of these questions -- we cannot answer them fully -- we shall point out how traditional neoclassical theory helps in defining the question, but must be extended beyond its present scope to provide answers.

The discussion will begin by considering both public and private nonprofit organizations -- i.e., all types of organizations except firms -- and then

1

will progressively narrow to certain types of private nonprofit enterprise. Since the study of nonprofit enterprise is at the frontier of public finance, grants economics, comparative economic systems, and "social economics" in general, we shall draw on a number of different perspectives as we proceed.

Definitions

The first question on our list is: "What are nonprofit enterprises?" Let us here take as a primitive term the word "enterprise," indicating only that it refers to a set of (human) individuals and a set of more or less clearly defined relationships among them. A synonym for "enterprise" is the term "organization."

For present purposes we distinguish two types of enterprise. A "profit enterprise" is an organization at least one of whose members has a property right (another primitive term) over a fraction of the difference between that organization's total revenue and total cost. Note that this definition says nothing about whether profits are maximized, only whether they can legitimately be made. Profit enterprises are also called "firms."

All other organizations are called "nonprofit enterprises" [Clarkson, 1980, p. ix; Hansmann, 1980, p. 838]. This usage is broader than that often used elsewhere; it encompasses a great variety of organizational forms: government, households, foundations, libraries, unions, mutual insurance companies, clubs, and many others. (In Chapter III a taxonomy of profit and nonprofit organizations is presented.) They all have in common the fact that they are not "owned" by anyone in the same sense as are firms; even though sometimes their leaders might behave as if they were owners, they are not allowed by law to admit it [Clarkson, 1980, pp. 17-18; Etzioni, 1976].

The first major distinction to be made within this general category is the distinction between public and private nonprofit enterprises. A public nonprofit enterprise is here conceived as an organization which is allowed to obtain some of its revenue by involuntary grants. The enterprise is usually called a "government" and the grants "taxation." National, provincial, and local governments fall into this category as do special-purpose districts with taxing power. Regional councils of governments without the power to assess mandatory dues on their members do not qualify, however, nor does the United Nations. Such organizations fall into a kind of shady area between public and private (see Chapter III), but we shall hereafter class them as private due to their lack of taxing power.

The second major distinction is between households (including kinship groups in general) and other private nonprofit organizations. We are now left with a group we can call "private nonprofit enterprises." They are private and are thus not governments; they are nonprofit and are thus not firms. They are not organized primarily for the purpose of consumption and internal redistribution and are thus not households.

It is clear that there are still many different types of organizations included in this category; examples would include the Ford Foundation, the Episcopal Church, Goodwill Industries, the Socialist Workers Party, and the public-interest groups of Ralph Nader and his followers. Note that an organization such as a "sheltered workshop" for the handicapped is included in our definition of a private nonprofit enterprise even though it sells some of its products in a market at nonzero prices. Whether or not it is self-supporting, the workshop provides services to its workers which a firm would not provide except as an in-kind wage. These services might be in the form of special work facilities made for the handicapped, counselling or vocational rehabilitation, or perhaps simply the chance to work at a job which no other organization is willing to provide. All these are part of the output of the workshop, sold to the worker at a zero price. (In the case of provision of the chance to work at a job, the chance has a zero price; the job itself is an exchange relation.)

Overview

We have now answered the first question: "What are nonprofit enterprises?" The next three chapters answer the rest of the questions.

The second question on our list is: "What do nonprofit enterprises do?" Chapter II answers this question by drawing on the work of Richard A. Musgrave in public finance. Musgrave [1959, Chapter 1; 1980, Chapter 1] classifies the economic activities of government into three "functions": allocation, distribution, and stabilization. These categories correspond to the three conventional branches of modern economic theory. "Microeconomics" includes the first two (Musgrave's work has a general-equilibrium orientation where necessary, so that it is not a separate category), and "macroeconomics" concerns itself with the third. Most textbooks in economic theory are organized in such a way that these categories are mutually exclusive and exhaustive.

Since Musgrave confines himself to the analysis of government fiscal policy, these categories are sufficient as a first approximation. However, when the scope of attention is expanded to include all activities of government, and when we expand further to include activities of other nonprofit enterprises, two new categories are needed. The first category is the "environmental" and the second is the "systemic." Both their definitions and their placement in logical progression are important.

For a scientific model to be tractable, certain variables must be held constant so that attention can be focused on the others. The variables held constant are called "parameters." In neoclassical microeconomics theory, parameters include taste, technology, and resource endowments. These constitute the environment of the economic system [Conn, 1978]. Yet the values of each of these have to be determined by some process. This process is the environmental function.

Tastes may be determined partly through advertising -- which is done through the economic system -- but primarily they are determined by the sociocultural (and perhaps political) environment and not by economic forces. The same socializing enterprises as before have a hand: households, schools, churches, government propaganda bureaus, and street gangs will help shape individual preferences. Clearly nonprofit enterprises have an important role here (one is tempted to say the dominant role), and market institutions -- advertising notwithstanding -- largely take tastes as given.

Much the same is true for technology when we

4

consider that advances in the basic sciences -- necessary before the innovations based on them can be made by firms -- often take place in universities and research institutes or under the auspices of government agencies.

Individual endowments of course are related to natural conditions and past market transactions (and they also depend on the society's property rights arrangements), but they can be rearranged through transfers, which can be voluntary or involuntary (the latter being through governments or gangs). Nonprofit enterprises and nonmarket institutions have a hand here too, not always susceptible to analysis by neoclassical methods.

The second function is the "systemic function" -- the setting of conditions under which market transactions can take place. The necessary conditions are "ownership," "trust," and "market information."

Before individuals can trade, they need a clear idea of what can be traded and by whom. Someone or something has to define what constitutes a tradeable commodity (not all "goods" or "economic goods" are tradeable), and what property rights link any particular commodity to a particular individual. Both law and custom are involved with both: U.S. law says I may not consider heroin a tradeable commodity, and certain religious traditions say the same for consecrated wine. Markets <u>cannot</u> be used in the process of defining tradeability, since the process determines when markets are appropriate. Therefore we expect firms not to be involved in this, since they are appropriate forms of organization mainly for making market transactions, and we are not surprised to see nonprofit enterprises (governments, churches) to be involved here. Thus the usual neoclassical theory of the firm and market is clearly out of place in this territory.

Market participants must also have a certain minimum of trust that transactions will be carried out in accordance with their wishes -- i.e., that contracts will be honored. In some circumstances they can simply trust each other: they have been socialized (by family, school, or church) into behaving honestly themselves and into believing that other market participants will do the same. In other cases they may place their trust in a third party --

5

usually a government -- to enforce the contract if necessary. Thus two types of activity, economic socialization and contract enforcement, are performed to induce trust, and nonprofit enterprises are involved in both types of activity.

Market information (i.e., knowledge of price and product quality and of other market actors) is not always easily acquired, especially in markets that cover large geographic areas or for products that result from sophisticated technology. Some nonprofit enterprises provide individuals with the "full" information that neoclassical theory often assumes they already have.

These first two functions are logically prior to the neoclassical model -- they include activities which are assumed to have been performed before the market begins. Therefore using the neoclassical model of firms and markets to analyze such activities constitutes using a model to analyze its own assumptions.

The next three functions include activities which ideally step in when the market fails to operate properly. They are logically "simultaneous with" or "subsequent to" market activity, but they involve actions in the absence of a market or actions to modify market solutions.

The third economic function is allocation. Nonprofit enterprises engage in activities to correct market failures, real or only perceived, in four areas: (i) they allocate public goods and goods subject to externalities (or "reallocate" through taxation or other means), (ii) they regulate price, quantity, or quality when markets are subject to imperfections, (iii) they encourage (or engage in) production of "merit goods" and discourage that of "demerit goods," and (iv) they modify market determination of risk and time differentials. Public and private nonprofit enterprises both have a hand in all of these, though governments can be expected to figure more prominently. Neoclassical theory has a long tradition in (i) and (ii) [see any standard intermediate microeconomics text for chapters on welfare economics and imperfect competition respectively] and in the public finance of (iv) [Musgrave, 1976], and there is actually little to say about (iii) in general. However, the focus has been "normative" rather than "positive" in (i) and (iv); there has been more concern with how to determine the "proper" allocation than with whether anyone in the government or elsewhere has the incentive to try to reach it. Public-choice theory has begun to shift the focus in recent years [Mueller, 1976, 1979], but there still is a long way to go -- especially for private nonprofit enterprises.

The fourth function is distribution, which is the modification of individual endowments through activities in the current period. Redistribution, either in cash or in kind, can be performed by households (within them or between them), charities, or governments in the same way that endowments are modified in the second function. Neoclassical methods have been used to describe redistribution by individuals [Collard, 1978; Hochman, 1969, 1970], and to generate normative criteria for such redistribution through governments [Musgrave, 1976], but there exists no positive theory of redistribution through charity enterprises.

The fifth economic function of nonprofit enterprise is the stabilizational function. The "neoclassical synthesis" of Keynesian and classical macroeconomics was designed to provide governments with a guide to the consequences of fiscal and monetary policy, but there the government itself is treated as an exogenous entity [Branson, 1972; Musgrave, 1976]. There is only recently emerging a positive neoclassical theory of, for example, government economic behavior over the business cycle. [See Frey, 1978, Chapters 10 and 11.]

The importance of focusing attention on government is of course that there is only one national government in an economy and it can therefore (in principle at least) act with a consistent purpose. Presumably in an economy with a relatively weak government and a relatively strong single household (the royal family in a developing kingdom?) or private nonprofit enterprise (a religious hierarchy in a theocracy?), it might be necessary to develop a theory of stabilization policy of another sort. However, even in an economy such as the U.S., we might consider the question of whether nonprofit enterprises are net stabilizers or destabilizers, taking into account not just their financial situation but their overall effect on the economy.

The interrelation of the different functions is of fundamental importance in evaluating the performance of nonprofit enterprises. However, the point here is that once we begin including such questions as the effect on economic growth of a decrease in trust or an increase in the speed of communication among market participants, we leave the field of neoclassical economics as traditionally defined, yet these are the kinds of trade-offs that must be evaluated consciously or unconsciously by society as a whole.

Chapter III addresses the third and fourth questions: "Why are nonprofit enterprises created?" and "How do they operate?" It is argued that nonprofit enterprises differ from firms both in the motivations behind their creation and in the constraints under which they operate.

There are three general types of organizations in the economy: public nonprofit enterprises (governments, special purpose districts, etc.), private nonprofit enterprises (foundations, clubs, etc.), and profit enterprises (corporations, cooperatives, etc.). In addition, however, organizations in each of these categories can be classified as entrepreneurial or associational, depending on how centralized the formal policy-making arrangements are within the organization. Individuals in the economy are thus faced with (and help to create) not only the choice of which economic activities to perform, but also the choice of organizational arrangements within which to perform them.

It can thus be expected that some of the motivations of individuals can be the same across all types of organization, and some can differ substantially from one organizational type to another. In all organizations we may find, for example, motives of self-perpetuation, self-protection, self-expansion, self-challenge, or even self-sacrifice. We may also find certain other organizational characteristics throughout all types: separation of ownership (membership, etc.) from control, satisficing behavior, X-inefficiency, and group-choice decision problems within the organization (e.g., voting paradoxes on the board of trustees). The differences between profit and nonprofit enterprises thus cannot be explained by reference to these type of problems.

It is argued here, however, that there are motivations which do differ across organizational types, and that these are causes and not effects of decisions by individuals to act through a particular organizational type. For situations in which people's goals are primarily selfish -- e.g., a desire to earn income in order to purchase commodities that enter into the utility function as private goods -- the firm is the logical type to use. On the other hand, if the motive is to produce a public good under conditions that avoid a free-rider problem, a government may be the type more often considered appropriate. If the motive is to redistribute income in kind to supercede the preferences of another individual deemed incapable of forming satisfactory ones on its own (say, feeding an infant or derelict), then a household or private nonprofit enterprise might be chosen. (Such motives are further explored in the appendix.) In all these cases except the firm, the goal is not primarily to generate income but to accomplish some task. In other words, the output of the organization is important independently of the income earned by the sale of that output -- in fact, the output is important whether or not it earns any income at all. Thus the distinction between profit and nonprofit enterprises is paritally concerned with the difference between producing output for profit and performing a task for other purposes. The answer to the third question then, is that nonprofit enterprises are created for what they do, not what they earn. Consequently their earnings cannot be used as an indicator of success. However, this leaves open the question of how to evaluate what they do, which is considered in the preceding chapters.

The choice is not simply between profit and nonprofit enterprises. Within the nonprofit category the choice must be made between public and private organizations. What governs the choice between public and private? Chapter III argues that the primary consideration would be the degree to which the free-rider problem is considered important by the individuals making the choice.

The fourth question is: "How do nonprofit enterprises operate?" More specifically, how do the constraints under which they operate differ from those to which firms are subject? Chapter III discusses three areas in which such differences might exist: external constraints, target group, and internal constraints. As in the case of motivations, there are many constraints that operate in organizations regardless of type, but some constraints differ between profit, public nonprofit, and private nonprofit enterprises. [Clarkson emphasizes this: 1980, pp. 3-27.] It is argued that those differences are often either bound up with the nature of nonprofitness itself or are the result of attempts by society through the legal system, or by the controlling group of the enterprise, to incorporate nonselfish incentives in the organization by either supplementing, coinciding with, or superseding selfish ones.

The external constraints include the capital market and the government. Nonprofit enterprises as a group have a different relationship to the capital market than do firms. They can sometimes borrow, but they of course cannot sell stock. They can, however, often solicit donations, a practice which if undertaken by a firm is likely to be futile, if not forbidden.

The government affects all enterprises in various ways, from creating the rules under which they are organized (including itself through constitutional law) to regulation to taxation. Chapter III discusses how taxes influence the operation of private nonprofit enterprises and asks what rationale might govern tax policy toward them.

The target group consists of the clientele, who receive the services of the organization, and the donors, who provide its revenue. In the case of firms, the two groups coincide and are its customers; in the case of nonprofit enterprises they are wholly or partly separated.

Problems of internal organization and accounting exist in any enterprise, but profits provide the firm with a single guide in arranging its activities. Profit is at once a success indicator, an incentive system, and a signalling device for resource movement, not only for the organization as a whole but often internally, through use of "profit centers," transfer pricing, and the like. No such single guide exists for nonprofit enterprises. Not only are all three roles split, but some are not even measurable --at least not at present. Chapter III considers the implications of this problem, both for the internal organization of nonprofit enterprises and for their accounting systems.

The last question on our list is: "How well do nonprofit enterprises perform?" Economists separate this into two questions for the firm: "How well is the firm producing its current level of output?" and "Is its current level of output worth producing?" These are Boulding's fourth and fifth marginal conditions for a social optimum [1952, Table 1]: the first asks if each firm is operating on its own expansion path for a given level of output, and the second asks whether the given level of output is correct. In the second chapter it is argued that the latter question often cannot be answered within the scope of conventional neoclassical theory. Chapter IV attempts to answer the first within that scope.

The are several ways of approaching this question. The first is to claim that nonprofit enterprises are merely closet firms: they maximize profits in fact if not in name, and therefore the theory of the firm applies to them nearly as well as to firms, after allowing for the distortions necessary to get around the law. The disadvantage of this approach is that it raises the question of why anyone interested in profits would establish a nonprofit enterprise in the first place.

The second approach is to claim that the neoclassical theory of production and cost is applicable as is, since "cost-effectiveness analysis" and other techniques show the nonprofit enterprise how to operate on its expansion path, and the profit motive only serves to show which point on the path the firm should follow. "Cost-benefit analysis" can then approximate the profit motive by showing the nonprofit enterprise where to operate, and a unique solution is found. The problem with this approach is that is again raises the question of why anyone in a nonprofit enterprise would be interested in either cost-effectiveness or cost-benefit analysis anyway: what incentive would the manager have to operate on the enterprise's expansion path, much less choose a point on that path that meets some criterion of maximum net social benefit? The "normative" question may be answered, but the "positive" one is not.

The third approach is to attack the question of motivation directly and see if neoclassical theory has something to say about it. If the enterprise manager is not allowed to maximize profits, does the manager maximize anything else? The ready answer is a

11

managerial utility function with arguments that are appropriate to the manager's relation to the enterprise. Thus, the neoclassical method can be used at the enterprise level for nonprofit enterprises without treating them as firms in disguise. The use of a managerial-utility function can help to answer the question of whether the enterprise has an incentive to operate on its expansion path.

Chapter IV takes precisely this approach: the enterprise is assumed to be headed by a manager who maximizes a utility function that is defined over the manager's consumption, labor, job amenities (fancy desks, expense accounts, etc.), and the output of the enterprise. First-order conditions are derived which indicate that, in a limited way, the enterprise indeed produces its output efficiently.

Clearly, then the "economics of nonprofit enterprise" is too broad a field for "neoclassical economic theory" to cover adequately. We have seen, however, that there are ways in which neoclassical theory has been helpful. Accordingly, we find that it is of great value but has limited usefulness in answering the five major questions we have asked about it.

After a long period of neglect, the serious study of nonprofit enterprise has begun to emerge from several directions within economics. Empirical work in related areas, such as health, education, and social services, has been going on for some time. It is time now to begin work on a single theoretical basis for the economics of nonprofit enterprise that is as rich and versatile as the theory of the firm. That is the central goal of this study.

CHAPTER II

THE NONMARKET SECTORS IN THE ECONOMIC SYSTEM

Introduction

When we begin to look at the outputs of public and private nonprofit organizations, a curious thing happens. We begin to discover that their "outputs" are far more complicated than those of most firms -- sometimes of a wholly different nature in their relationship to the economic system and its participants. Many of these organizations exist to perform the difficult tasks that firms either avoid (as too difficult or unprofitable, though perhaps necessary) or take for granted. These tasks often are assumed in traditional neoclassical theory to have been carried out by someone "before" (logically, though not chronologically) firms and markets begin to operate.

Thus neoclassical methods may be adequate for looking at the input side of nonprofit enterprises -- after all, their activities require the use of real resources -- but are wholly inadequate for looking at the output side. They may be not only inadequate, but illogical and misleading if used to evaluate the "efficiency" or "optimality" of the output of many nonprofit enterprises.

This chapter will describe the output of public and private nonprofit organizations as functions they perform in the economy. Both types are included here because the discussion is general enough to apply to all nonprofit enterprises. As the argument proceeds, it will be claimed that the neoclassical framework fits into a larger whole -- and that use of it to evaluate matters outside its scope may lead to logical circularities or inappropriate answers. Our assumption here is, however, that an extension of economic analysis to incorporate a larger frame of reference will be a start toward finding whatever methods of evaluation lie out there to be discovered.

Nonprofit Enterprise and Neoclassical Economics

Neoclassical economic theory has had very little

to say about private nonprofit enterprises. For example, apparently only one graduate-level textbook in microeconomics mentions them at all [Nicholson, 1978, pp. 276-277]. By contrast, the neoclassical theory of the firm has been well developed for decades [e.g., Hicks, 1946, Chapters VI and VII], and the positive and normative extensions of the profit-maximization hypothesis are now standard in graduate textbooks [Henderson, 1980, Chapter 4; Varian, 1978, Chapter 1]. The economic theory of government behavior has only recently begun to emerge from its largely normative public-finance origins into a more complete positive and normative system [Frey, 1978; Mueller, 1979].

The study of private nonprofit enterprises has lagged behind this. There has been some activity, and it is growing, but it is still rather scattered among different subfields of economics and different industries in which they may predominate. Nevertheless, there have been only a handful of attempts to look at private nonprofit enterprises in general [Clarkson, 1980; Ginzberg, 1965; Weisbrod, 1977; Young, 1983]. There has not arisen a consensus as yet on the proper formulation of a theory of the private nonprofit enterprise. Some ideas are inconsistent with each other; some pieces of the puzzle are missing altogether.

Any field as new as the economics of nonprofit enterprise can expect a piecemeal development for a while as different gaps are seen and closed up. However, there is a fundamental reason why this field in particular can have such a confusing development: that reason is rooted in the restrictive assumptions of neoclassical theory [Graaff, 1971, Chapter X; Koopmans, 1957, p. 44].

The assumptions are not often completely and explicitly specified; many times an assumption will surface in an author's writing only when the author is ready to violate it [for example, Hirshleifer, 1980, Chapter 17. Moreover, not all assumptions which are specified are restrictive (i.e., are necessary in order for the conclusions to follow). Nevertheless, it is possible to draw up a list of the assumptions upon which neoclasical economic theory rests. The following list of restrictive neoclassical assumptions groups them into categories which will be useful in the rest of this chapter:

14

1. **Environmental**

    a. <u>Tastes</u>. Preferences are strictly concave (or indifference curves convex), exogenous, and constant. Individuals choose the most-preferred opportunity. [Bator, 1957, p. 456; Baumol, 1977, pp. 218-220; Becker, 1976, p. 5; Graaff, 1971, p. 147; Samuelson, 1980, p. 44; Shepherd, 1979, p. 37].

    b. <u>Technology</u>. Production isoquants are convex, and technology exhibits constant returns to scale and is exogenous and constant [Bator, 1957, p. 456; 1958, pp. 528- 31; Samuelson, 1980, p.44; Shepherd, 1979, p. 37].

    c. <u>Resource Endowments</u>. The economy's stock of resources is exogenous and constant, and the endowments of each participant have been determined from the distribution (and redistribution) of income in the last period [Bator, 1957, p. 456; Samuelson, 1980, p. 44, cf Graaff, 1971, p. 144]. Each participant has an endowment upon which he or she can survive whether or not exchange takes place [Koopmans, 1957, pp. 55, 59, 62].

2. **Systemic**

    a. <u>Ownership</u>. Private property-rights constraints have been determined exogenously and unambiguously over all economic goods and bads [cf. Bator, 1958, in Breit, 1971, pp. 526-528].

    b. <u>Trust</u>. The level of trust among participants is sufficiently high that they believe their contracts will be honored [Freidman, 1970, p. 52; Arrow, 1974]. That is,

15

no theft [Mueller, 1979, Chapter 1].

c. <u>Market Information</u>. There is perfect knowledge of price and quality of every output and input by every relevant market participant [Shepherd, 1979, p. 37].

3. **Allocative**

a. <u>Public Goods, Externalities</u>.
There are no public or quasi-public goods, and there are no external costs or benefits [Bator, 1957, p. 456; 1958, pp. 531-532; Shepherd, 1979, p. 37].

b. <u>Competition</u>. All goods and services are traded in perfectly-competitive markets, i.e., all participants are price takers and all resources are perfectly mobile [Samuelson, 1980, p. 44; Shepherd, 1979, p. 37].

c. <u>Merit and Demerit Goods</u>. There are no merit or demerit goods [Musgrave, 1959, pp. 9, 13-14; 1980, pp. 84-86].

d. <u>Intertemporal Relationships</u>. There is no excessive risk or uncertainty and there is no divergence between private and social discount rates. [Graaff, 1971, p. 143; Musgrave, 1980, pp. 188-189].

An economy in which all these assumptions hold and which finds its market all in long-run equilibrium will have met the Pareto criterion for allocative efficiency [Samuelson, 1980, p. 44]. That is, there is no way in which the economy could reallocate its resources to make any participant better off without making at least one other participant worse off. This is the significance of these assumptions.

As is well known, there is no guarantee that if these assumptions hold the economy will meet any criteria other than allocative efficiency. For example, there is no guarantee that the distribution of income will be equitable [Bator, 1957, pp. 460-461, 464-465; Graaff, 1971, p. 150] or even that all participants will survive to the end of the period [Koopmans, 1957, p. 59].

As is also well known, if any of these assumptions is violated, the market process by itself cannot even guarantee an efficient allocation (since the restrictions are restrictive) [Bator, 1957, 1958; Hirshleifer, 1980, pp. 529-544]. If the allocative assumptions are violated, the market will allocate resources inefficiently; if either an environmental or systemic assumption is violated, there may not be a market at all. Thus the economic system idealized in this model relies on its sociopolitical environment to insure its efficient operation.

Public and private nonprofit enterprises straddle the economic system and its environment. Set up mostly for "noneconomic" reasons, they nevertheless affect the economic system even in the idealized neoclassical version by creating the conditions under which the assumptions are satisfied or by making changes in the outcome of the system when they are not.

Moreover, nonprofit enterprises themselves are a result of the alteration of property rights; by definition their existence violates assumption 2a. Therefore any economic model that incorporates nonprofit enterprises into its analysis must extend beyond the restrictive boundaries of neoclassical theory both in its positive analysis and its selection of normative performance criteria.

In the next section we outline the activities of nonprofit enterprises, classifying them in relation to the assumptions of the neoclassical model. In the section after that we discuss the necessity for extending economic analysis beyond the neoclassical framework to account for and evaluate these activities.

The Economic Functions of Nonprofit Enterprise

Weisbrod [1977, Chapter 3] and Levitt [see

17

McGill and Wooten, 1975, pp. 444-445] attempt to explain private nonprofit enterprises as supplements to firms. Weisbrod explains them as supplements to governments in the production of certain types of goods. Levitt sees them as either assuming tasks which governments and firms cannot or will not do well enough, or as attempting to transform those organizations into ones which will do a better job themselves.

The idea of nonprofit enterprises as supplements may be adequate as a partial explanation, but it is not a complete one. For one thing, our definition of "nonprofit enterprise" is more inclusive than those of Weisbrod or Levitt: we include governments under that definition. For another thing, nonprofit enterprises of both these types predate firms by hundreds, even thousands, of years. It is modern firms which have taken over areas previously under the jurisdiction of nonprofit enterprises in the last several centuries in the West. Weisbrod [1972, p. 60] points out that the question of who supplements whom is not important, but rather the question of the mix of enterprise types performing different tasks.

In order to get a clear picture of this mix, we must describe what it is that nonprofit enterprises do. Richard A. Musgrave classifies the fiscal activities of governments into the three "functions" of allocation, distribution, and stabilization [Musgrave, 1959, Chapter 1; Musgrave and Musgrave, 1976, Chapter 1]. Kenneth Boulding [1973, pp. 7-9] describes these same categories (he calls the third one "development," which is a significant generalization of Musgrave) as the functions of the grants economy. These three categories of course correspond to the three divisions of economic theory, the first two from microeconomics and the third from macroeconomics.

However, the activities of organizations, especially those as diverse as nonprofit enterprises, are too varied to be captured in these categories. Many nonprofit enterprises are created for purposes not seen as traditionally "economic," yet their activities affect the economy in ways other than simply the fact that they use up real resources in producing output. In addition to allocation, distribution, and stabilization, governments and private nonprofit organizations perform at least two other functions

18

essential to the economy: an "environmental" function (the setting of the parameters economists usually hold constant in their models), and a "systemic"
function (the setting of the conditions under which
market transactions take place).

Actually, firms also engage in activities that
fit within these categories, but their role is much
smaller. There is considerable overlap in the functions performed by different types of organization.
We cannot therefore assume a tight division of labor
as does Musgrave [1959, pp. 5-6] when he pretends
that the government can have a "Fiscal Department"
with three "Branches," each of which has a manager
in charge of one function. We must proceed in a manner more like Weisbrod [1978, p. 70], who, for other
reasons, assumes that all three types of organization
(firm, government, and private nonprofit enterprises)
may be doing the same things, but that one type will
predominate in one area and another in another.

Both Boulding [1973, pp. 7-9] and Musgrave
[1959, pp. 4-5] claim that the allocative, distributive, and stabilizational functions are performed simultaneously; Boulding goes on to assert that they
are mutually interdependent. However, most textbooks
in microeconomics put allocation first and make distribution theory depend on theories of "derived demand." The "microfoundations" approach in macroeconomics emphasizes what we have known all along, which
is that our macro models are based on assumptions
about micro behavior more than the other way around.
Thus even though in reality "everything in interdependent," in our economic models there is a logical order to the three economic functions: allocation is
done "first," then distribution is "next," and stabilization is "last."

In any case, the two additional functions fit
into economic theory at the very beginning -- in the
assumptions. In the previous section we listed those
assumptions under the categories of "environmental"
and "systemic," and we indicated where they fit into
the theoretical structure.

Thus the discussion of the economic functions
of nonprofit enterprise follows the logical sequence
in which the topics they cover fit into conventional
economic theory: environmental, systemic, allocative, distributive, and stabilizational. Though

there are overlaps and interactions among different functions, the importance of this logical sequence for the use of economic analysis in evaluating the performance of nonprofit enterprise will be pointed out in the next section.

One point should be made before we proceed. The use of the term "function" in this chapter is not intended to imply that we are taking a particular sociological point of view -- though our discussion would probably be more compatible with some ("functionalism" or "conflict functionalism") than with others ("dialectical conflict theory," interaction theory") [see Turner, 1974, Chapters 3, 6, 7, 9].

The Environmental Function

In neoclassical general-equilibrium analysis, certain assumptions have explicit mathematical interpretations. The main distinction between activities in the environmental and systemic categories is that the former show up in models as parameters (variables held constant for the purpose of analysis) whereas the latter, if they are even stated, do not show up in the formal analysis at all.

Households and other private nonprofit enterprises (such as churches, youth groups, colleges, and clubs) help to shape individual preferences for various mixes of goods and services. This activity is distinguished from the delineation of commodities described below, though it is closely related to it.

Firms do engage in advertising in an attempt to change tastes, but it is in most cases only to shift brand loyalties; it is only in industries which are relatively close to being perfectly competitive that an industry-wide effort attempts to change tastes toward the "generic" output itself.

Scherer [1980, pp. 410-411] describes the role of nonprofit enterprise in technological change in the United States:

> Basic research, defined as investigation to gain knowledge for its own sake, consumed 3 percent of all industrial R and D outlays in 1975. Applied research, investigation directed toward obtaining

20

knowledge into specific commercial implications, accounted for 19 percent of total spending. The remaining 78 percent went into _development_, that is, the translation of technical and scientific knowledge into concrete new products and processes. Private industry accounts for roughly 17 percent of all basic research conducted in the United States, 55 percent of all applied research, and 85 percent of all development. From these figures it is evident that industry's forte is applications -- specific new products and processes -- while pure science remains predominately the domain of the universities and federal government laboratories. [Emphasis in original.]

Technological change thus ultimately stems from basic research, but firms do not generally enter the process except at the applied-research and development stages. Thus it is nonprofit enterprises which are ultimately responsible for the shifting out of society's production possibilities. (Perhaps the firms stay out because of the risk due to the long time horizon that science, rather than engineering, has. Firms are interested only in success; scientists can also be fascinated by failures.)

Particular types of "risky" long-term basic research may be the comparative advantage of private universities rather than ones which are government bureaus. State legislators may resemble firms in their look for a quick, practical payoff where patience and tolerance for unorthodoxy are more appropriate.

It is not always made explicit in economics textbooks that the initial distribution of resources among society's members (i.e., their wealth) is a datum for the analysis of the current period; Nicholson [1978, pp. 658-659] and Wonnacott [1979, pp. 188-189] are perhaps the best exceptions. [See also Bator, 1957, p. 465; and Musgrave, 1980, p. 102.] Musgrave [1959, p. 19] points out:

The difficulty is to decide what the proper state of distribution should be. The decision evidently cannot be made by a market process, since the nature of

exchange presupposes title to the things
that are to be exchanged. A political process of decision making is needed, and before this can function, there must be some
distribution of weights in the political
process.

Weisbrod [July, 1978] would presumably agree, but
only after adding private nonprofit enterprises as
possible participants.

Changes in the distribution of income and
wealth are partly determined by current market transactions, but public and private nonprofit enterprises, through their distributive functions discussed
below, influence in one period the endowments of individuals in the next.

The Systemic Function

Those activities concerned with setting the conditions under which market transactions take place
("the rules of the game") are classified under the
"systemic function." Traditional neoclassical theory
does not deal with these activities explicitly, since
they are assumed to have been completed at the outset
of the period under consideration. Economists in the
fields of public choice, property-rights theory, and
the theory of economic systems are entering the study
of this area, but there are still gaps in research
[Mueller, 1976, 1979; Furubotn, 1974; Conn, 1978].

In the carrying out of these activities there
is some division of labor here among governments,
households, and other organizations. However, several types participate in carrying out a number of
these activities.

Ownership

The delineation of what constitutes an exchangeable commodity and the determination of who is allowed to do the exchanging are activities which must
take place before the actual exchange can occur.
However, the results of such activities vary from one
society to another and, over time, within the same
society.

Certain human beings of African descent were

delineated as (exchangeable) commodities in Europe
and North America until the last century. This was
both by law (government) and by custom (churches and
households). Through a combination of efforts by a
wide range of nonprofit enterprises, both law and custom were changed. The enterprises involved in the
change included churches, political action groups,
households (families who taught antislavery ideas to
their children), and of course governments (through
their armies, chiefs of state, and legislators).

The subject of property rights is a topic which
has grown in popularity among economists in recent
years. Government action has largely replaced custom
and tradition (through households and other groups)
in the determination of such rights. A view on why
governments may have the comparative advantage in
this area is provided by Arrow [1974, in Phelps,
1975, p. 24]:

> More basic yet, I will say, is the
> idea that the price system, in order to
> work at all, must involve the concept of
> property (even in the socialistic state
> there is public property). Property sys-
> tems are in general not completely self-
> enforcing. They depend for their defini-
> tion upon a constellation of legal proce-
> dures, both civil and criminal. The course
> of the law itself cannot be regarded as sub-
> ject to the price system. The judges and
> the police may indeed be paid, but the sys-
> tem itself would disappear if on each oc-
> casion they were to sell their services and
> decisions. Thus the definition of property
> rights based on the price system depends
> precisely on the lack of universality of
> private property and of the price sys-
> tem. . . . The price system is not, and
> perhaps in some basic sense cannot be, uni-
> versal. To the extent that it is incom-
> plete, it must be supplemented by an implic-
> it or explicit social contract. Thus one
> might loosely say that the categorical im-
> perative and the price system are essential
> complements.

Trust

Arrow also has some interesting things to say

23

about trust [1974, p. 23]:

> Consider what is thought of as a high-
> er or more elusive value than pollution or
> roads: trust among people. Now trust has
> a very important pragmatic value, if noth-
> ing else. Trust is an important lubricant
> of a social system. It is extremely effi-
> cient; it saves a lot of trouble to have
> a fair degree of reliance on other people's
> word. Unfortunately this is not a commodi-
> ty which can be bought very easily. If you
> have to buy it, you already have some
> doubts about what you've bought.

Households, other private nonprofit enterprises
(e.g., churches), and government bureaus (e.g., public schools) all participate in the process of in-
stilling trust and trustworthy behavior. However,
they differ in the activities they perform in this
regard. There are at least two types of activity:
economic socialization and contract enforcement.

Most lying, cheating, and theft are probably
prevented, long before they have a chance to occur,
through the activity we can call "economic socialization," the training of individuals in the type of behavior expected of them in the marketplace. Most
customers in restaurants would pay the bill whether
or not they believed they would be caught and prose-
cuted otherwise. (One reason we know this is that
waitresses and waiters still rely on tips and on the
infrequency of persons who walk out without paying;
the waitress or waiter is liable for the bill in most
restaurants.)

The type of behavior exhibited by trustworthy
people lowers the risks and the transaction costs to
all members of society the more of those people there
are. In some professions this kind of trustworthy
behavior is quite important because it is closely related to the market-information activity discussed
below.

All three major types of nonprofit enterprise
participate in economic socialization to some degree.
Households of course are involved with training children, and churches also participate. Public schools,
however, also have a hand in the process.

When economic socialization fails to produce uni-
versal compliance with the standards of trust set by
the society for economic transactions, the government
stands ready to fill in through its role as enforcer
of contracts. This is the systemic trust-producing
activity in which the government has a comparative
advantage through its courts and monopoly on legiti-
mated violence. There are, however, other types of
organizations involved, such as civil-rights legal-
action groups or consumer-oriented watchdog organizations.

Market Information

The opportunity set of an individual or organization properly includes only opportunities that are
known; it is impossible to make a decision about a
course of action one does not know is possible.
Therefore information on market conditions (price and
quality) can be treated as a determinant of the opportunities faced by firms and individuals. Since the
flow and cost of market information are to a large
extent determined by the characteristics of the economic system [Conn, 1978; Neuberger and Duffy, 1976],
the activities related to market information are considered part of the systemic function.

Two closely-related but distinct subjects should
be distinguished here also. The information aspects
of economic behavior are often known by the misnomer
"economics of information." The economic aspects of
information and knowledge -- a fascinating subject
that overlaps with many fields including computer
science and library science -- is another field, properly seen as a branch of the study of the allocation
function mentioned below. What is the difference?
The first category includes only market information;
information on all other subjects is in the second
category.

Examples of the provision of market information
by nonprofit enterprises abound: the Federal Government generates the Consumer Price Index, Consumers
Union collects and disseminates information on many
products by brand name, libraries provide access to
the first two.

Of course all this information must be in a language that can be understood by the market participants. There are many examples of "trade languages,"

spoken by key merchants which facilitate exchange over a wide area, or among people of very different backgrounds. Some of these languages may have been developed by traders themselves: e.g., pidgen in China and the South Sea Islands, and Hausa in Africa, and lingua franca in the Mediterranean [Pei, 1965, pp. 244, 439]. Others are based on one or more languages spoken by a group of people who do much of the trading themselves, e.g., Ladino or Yiddish among Jews. Much of the teaching of languages, even trade languages, can be expectd to be done through households and schools as well as the firms who use them.

Information about product quality has a lot to do with trust. Weisbrod [June, 1978, pp. 5-14] hypothesizes that one reason for the existence of non-profit enterprises is that they may be more trustworthy than firms (who have a clear profit incentive to lie if they can). Therefore they may predominate in areas where suppliers have more information on product quality than demanders, and where expertise is consequently needed to evaluate the quality of the good or service. It may also have to do with the potential risk to the demander: automobile dealers fit Weisbrod's criteria, but not so well as hospital emergency rooms.

The market-information activity is to some extent regulated by the ownership-determination activity through disclosure laws. [I owe this point to Jim Meehan.] If the Ford Motor Company must disclose market information on its assets, but the Ford Foundation does not, there may be effects on the feedback mechanism to the latter quite separate from its non-profit status. That is, inefficiencies in the grants mechanism may be traceable more to differences in the information flow than to the profitness or nonprofitness of the organizations involved.

The Allocative Function

Of the five economic functions discussed here, economists have been most interested in the allocative function. Indeed the most popular definitions of economics refer only to its study of the allocative function. As a consequence of this preoccupation with what is admittedly at the heart of the subject, economists have concentrated their attention on the behavior of firms and markets. However, nonprofit enterprises participate in markets and they also engage in activities which bypass markets and use some other mechanism for effecting or affecting the allocation of resources.

Public Goods and Externalities

Certain types of goods cannot be efficiently allocated through markets. Among these are so-called "public goods" [Bator, 1957, pp. 470-471; 1958, pp. 531-532]. From Collard [1978, p. 8] an alternative term might be "non-attributable goods," or ones whose services are consumed by all individuals at once and therefore are not attributable to any particular one of them.

Collard point out [1978, p. 8] that in the case of goods of this type, the distinction between benevolence and selfishness breaks down. Any individual who desires a certain quantity of the good for himself or herself knows that it will also be the same quantity enjoyed by another. This is an area of life where the commandment "love thy neighbor as thyself" is inescapable.

It is also true that in the means by which public goods are provided it is often quite difficult to separate selfish from "malevolent" -- or at least coercive -- motives. I vote to allow the government to coerce you and me to pay taxes for a good we both enjoy; here is a mixture of all three motives at once.

Economists usually think of governments as the allocators, but Weisbrod [1977, Chapter 3] claims private nonprofit enterprises can be suppliers of public goods. The reasoning is as follows. Suppose a 51 percent majority vote by all individuals sets the government output of a given public good at a particular level x. Suppose that there are a substantial number of voters who wanted a higher output x + y. They might band together to form a private nonprofit enterprise that would produce output level y, thus satisfying their demand. Weisbrod says nothing about the fact that this does not satify those minority voters who wanted a smaller government output; they are hurt even more in this case by the creation of the private nonprofit organization. If these voters band together and form a private nonprofit organization of their own, they could conceivably reduce output below x, but they would be using up real resources in the process.

There are other types of goods which are allocated by nonprofit enterprises. Another commonly-described source of market failure is the presence of external economies or diseconomies in consumption or production [Nicholson, 1978, Chapter 22]. The presence of externalities does not by itself lead to a breakdown of the market's ability to provide an efficient allocation [Collard, 1978, Chapter 2], but under the right conditions it can do just that. In the case of positive consumption externalities, which can be interpreted as benevolence, either public or private nonprofit enterprises may be efficient allocators, depending on the nature of the good in question.

Musgrave [1959, pp. 14-15] points out that the allocation ("provision") of a good is distinct from its production. In the case of government, he says that allocation means:

> simply, that the goods and services . . . must be paid for out of general revenues . . . at the same time, they need not be produced under the direct management or supervision of the government [p. 15, emphasis his].

The same distinction applies to private nonprofit enterprises. It also applies in reverse; if a firm pays a nonprofit enterprise to do a research project, for example, it is the firm that is determining how much research is provided to the economy.

An example of this distinction is given in Musgrave's discussion of lumpiness of imputs and decreasing cost of outputs [p. 7]. Such circumstances may make it impossible for a firm to produce efficiently without making a loss. "A tax-subsidy process -- and hence, budget policy -- is required to secure an optimal output." Here the firm still does the producing, but the government sets the level of output.

Regulation

In the presence of market imperfections, government action may correct market distortions through

28

various kinds of regulation of price or quality: an-
titrust action, price regulation, or the setting of
standards. It is difficult to see how private nonprofit enterprises can have any role in regulation
except as adjuncts to government: lobbying for or
against new regulations, participating in lawsuits,
etc. "Standards" or "seals of approval" coming from
private nonprofit charities have the character of market information, not quality regulation.

Merit and Demerit Goods

Certain goods deemed by "society" to be demanded
in too large or small quantities may be regulated,
prohibited, taxed, subsidized, or supplied by governments. Private nonprofit enterprises may also take
steps to provide merit goods (e.g., theatres, libraries, museums) or to try noncoercively to reduce the
supply of demerit goods (e.g., watchdog groups which
try to persuade networks to reduce violence on televi-
sion shows).

Musgrave [1959, pp. 13-14] does not speculate
as to the source of such "merit wants" or "demerit
wants" in the society, except to say that some groups
may be deemed to have greater knowledge about the benefits (or hazards) of certain goods and the rest of
us simply take their word for it. There is another
source, however:

> . . . some writers have tried to bring such
> objectives within the framework of individ-
> ualistic judgements, by extending the lat-
> ter to include views about the nature of
> society. Thus, a person may have private
> interest in reducing the tax on tobacco,
> since cigarettes enter importantly in his
> private utility function, but recognize in
> his social judgements that a reduction in
> cigarette consumption would be desirable.
> [Atkinson, 1980, p. 8]

The market reflects my (selfish) utility function for
the good itself, but my individual welfare function
includes preferences that can be expressed only outside the market. Thus the demand for merit goods (or
in this case the "negative demand" for "demerit
goods") can be expressed outside the market by the
same individuals who participate in the market.

Risk and Time

The discussion of public goods and merit goods can be extended over time to include risk and investment projects. Attempts by governments to invest according to a "social rate of discount" or what could be called a "social evaluation of risk" that differs from the one determined in the market are motivated by a mixture of these approaches [Musgrave, 1959, p. 7].

Private nonprofit enterprises also may be involved in this sort of activity. Museums and libraries, for example, make investments with very long time horizons, sometimes with effects that last for centuries after the government's public-works projects have washed away.

The Distributive Function

Markets provide for distribution of income only in relation to marginal product and market power. Nonprofit enterprises, either as a deliberate goal or as a byproduct often engage in redistribution activities. The necessity for this sort of activity to the survival of societies is pointed out by Boulding [1973, p. 9]:

> Any society, indeed, with no grants economy or a distribution-neutral grants economy would soon cease to exist, as its children would starve to death.

The determination of the proper distribution of income cannot be wholly divorced from the decision of how to bring it about. There are two types of redistribution mechanisms; redistribution in cash and redistribution in kind.

Collard [1978, pp. 122-123] points out that redistribution in cash is far less prevalent than one would expect. His context makes it clear that he refers only to redistribution among households, not within them. However, it is unclear whether inclusion of the latter would make a difference. In any event redistribution in cash has been a task undertaken with relish by governments in the last four decades, and Collard [p. 14] provides the rationale for why a private nonprofit enterprise -- at least a

30

small one -- may be reluctant to attempt this sort of redistribution: the effect is simply too small if spread over a large number of people.

The other type of distributive activity is redistribution in kind. According to Collard [1978, pp. 122-123], this has been by far the more popular type through the centuries. It seems that people are less interested in each other's happiness than in their consumption of specific goods. Private nonprofit enterprises are perhaps better suited for this type than for redistribution in cash, since it is easier for them to confine themselves to a specific set of roles, and also to measure what they are doing.

The Stabilizational Function

The stabilizational function is the macroeconomic aspect of economic behavior. It refers to activities which make it easier or more difficult for the economy "to maintain or achieve the goals of high employment, a reasonable degree of price level stability, balance in the foreign accounts, and an acceptable rate of economic growth" [Musgrave, 1980, p. 13].

National governments are usually the only single enterprises of any type large enough to have an impact on macroeconomic stability, though conceivably a multinational corporation, or even a large foundation [Asimov, 1951 1952, 1953], could affect the stability of a country. However, national governments are the only organizations with the full range of fiscal and monetary tools. Not even state and local governments have those capabilities.

Unfortunately, it would seem that private nonprofit enterprises might have a built-in destabilizing tendency. As the incomes of individuals and firms go down, they contribute less revenue to private nonprofit enterprises, which then decrease output and employment, the result of which is to pull incomes down further.

"Destabilization" may not necessarily be always bad: it depends on the direction it takes. It does not do a Third World country any good to be "stabilized" at a zero growth rate with a poverty level per capita GNP. A "destabilization" that would kick it

31

upward would be welcome in this case. However, the
kind of action that would cause such an event would
not properly be called destabilization, but rather
"development" [see Boulding, 1973, p. 9]. The reason
is that it would surely involve changes in the environmental and systemic activities carried on by nonprofit enterprises throughout that society, which
would make the entire economy evolve in a new direction.

The Evaluation of Nonprofit Enterprise

It is clear that nonprofit enterprises figure
prominently in many more types of economic activities
than do firms. In some cases they do things which
traditional neoclassical models assume have already
been done before the firms step in and the markets
begin to operate. In other cases they are set up precisely to make an end run around the market system.
This section will explore the implications of these
statements for economic analysis.

As mentioned before, even though in the real
world all five economic functions are performed con-
tinuously and simultaneously, traditional neoclassical theory clearly fits them into a logical sequence.
The conventional theory assumes that all environmental and systemic functions have been completed before
the analysis begins:

> Economic theory . . . discusses the
> use of given resources by given "owners,"
> in accord with a given system of technolo-
> gy, to satisfy given wants, all organized
> through a system of perfect markets. Any
> question as to what resources, technology,
> etc., are met with at a given time and
> place, must be answered in terms of institu-
> tional history, since all such things, in
> common with the impersonal system of market
> relations itself, are obviously culture-
> history facts and products. [Knight, 1921,
> p. xiv.]

The subject of microeconomics then is to analyze
the allocation and distribution functions and lay the
"microfoundations" for macroeconomics, whose jurisdiction is the stabilization function. Thus the logical
sequence implied here is from environmental and

systemic, to allocation and distribution, to stabilization, and each builds on the preceding. The environmental and systemic functions enter conventional economic theory only as assumptions. Though work has been done by economists in property rights [Furubotn, 1974], technological innovation [Heertje, 1973], and information [Lamberton, 1971] for example, their conclusions are still controversial -- sometimes even after decades of research -- due partly to the logical contradiction in using a model to analyze its own assumptions.

The preoccupation of economists with the study of firms at the organization level and with markets at the social-process level can perhaps be explained by the fact that the activities of firms and markets are overwhelmingly concerned with allocation and distribution under specific circumstances. However, economists are moving more into the study of nonprofit enterprises and nonmarket processes. Households and governments are no longer agents on the periphery; their internal decision making is of greater interest [Becker, 1976, Chapter 11; Mueller, 1976, Chapter 8; Niskanen, 1971]. Private nonprofit enterprises are also being studied more and more; among those types that have received attention in recent years are arts organizations [Hendon, 1980] and universities [Garvin, 1980].

The problem is that our criterion for evaluation of the efficiency of nonprofit enterprises is taken form the allocative function, whereas nonprofit enterprises are very often set up mostly to perform environmental, systemic, distributive, and even stabilizational functions. Therefore the criterion that economists use -- allocative efficiency -- is simply too narrow or even inappropriate to apply to public or private nonprofit enterprises, because it is based on a model of economic behavior that assumes away the problems that the enterprises in question are set up to solve.

Yet the criterion is of some relevance, and the tools of economic analysis are of use in describing and evaluating nonprofit enterprises. Those organizations use up real resources that could have been used elsewhere, and it is reasonable to ask whether they use them efficiently for maximum social welfare. The trouble is that at present our notions of "efficiency" and "welfare" are too narrow for us to analyze trade-offs between, say, resources devoted to systemic activities and resources used up in allocation, or between a systemic activity and one which shifts tastes or technology [Blaug, 1976, p. 17, mentions tastes in this light]. How many resources should be taken out of food production to help a country shift from a socialist to a capitalist economic system after a revolution? How clogged are we willing to let court dockets get in order to have more resources for religious evangelism? These choices involve shifting resources not merely from production of one good to another, but from performance of one function to performance of another.

Thus we cannot ask, for example, whether nonprofit enterprises choose an efficient level (or mix) of outputs. However, we can ask whether, to produce a given level (and mix) of output, the organization uses resources in an efficient manner. This is analogous to asking the question of whether a monopolist operated on its expansion path; an affirmative answer implies a kind of allocative efficiency on the input side, but says nothing about it on the output side. It obviously does not prevent us from finding the best way of doing something that should not be done at all [Boulding, 1973, p. 482]. However, it is the best we can do using neoclassical methods. This is the approach taken in Chapter IV, after we narrow our focus and describe the private nonprofit sector in more detail.

It is not within our scope here to suggest an extended efficiency or welfare criterion. However, some progress in this direction has been made. Boulding's work on evolution, grants economics, and human betterment [Boulding, 1973, and both 1977, 1978] are attempts to put "selfish" utility functions, firms, exchange transactions, and market institutions into a larger framework which includes nonprofit enterprises, threats and integrative transactions, and grants processes. Whether this and other work leads to an expanded criterion, or set of criteria, remains for the future to show. In the meantime, we should beware of fitting nonprofit enterprises too eagerly into our Procrustean normative categories. Until we have a sufficiently general set of criteria for evaluating the performance of all five economic functions, and until we know whether those criteria must include our present efficiency criteria as necessary conditions or whether there are trade-offs between those and other criteria, we should be wary of moving too quickly to praise or condemn the activities of nonprofit enterprises.

CHAPTER III

THE NATURE OF NONPROFIT ENTERPRISE

Introduction

The third and fourth questions on our list are: "Why are nonprofit enterprises created?" and "How do they operate?" Another way of stating these questions is to ask: "What are the goals and objectives of nonprofit enterprises (or, more properly, the individuals acting as members of them)?" and "What are the constraints under which they operate?"

Implicit in these questions is the assumption that their answers differ from what they are when we ask them about firms. After all, it is difficult to imagine an explanation for the existence of nonprofit organizations based on a description of ways in which they are exactly like firms.

In the first section we propose a three-dimensional taxonomy of all organizations, both profit and nonprofit, based on ownership (public nonprofit, private nonprofit, and private profit), governance (entrepreneural and associational), and financing (commerical, donative nonendowed, and donative endowed). All the categories are really points on continua, and there are organizations which fit in only as borderline cases.

The second section discusses goals and objectives of nonprofit organizations, in answer to question three. There are several aspects to the questions: are there goals which participants in any organization, profit or nonprofit, may have? Are there specific differences between the goals of firms, governments, and private nonprofit organizations (a question which may seem to have an obvious answer unless you are an economist)? In general, why would a society of economically rational individuals create all three major types of organization simultaneously?

The third discusses the types of constraints faced by nonprofit organizations -- external constraints (specifically, capital markets and governments), the target groups (for example, clients and donors), and internal constraints (specifically the relationship between the governing board and the

37

employees, and the accounting system).

The conclusion is that both goals and constraints differ between profit and nonprofit enterprises, and that differences in the latter sometimes are related to differences in the former.

Types of Economic Organizations

Most economists recognize four basic types of economic organizations: households, firms, governments, and private nonprofit enterprises. [Ginzburg, 1965, Chapter 1; Friedman, 1962, p. 7; Lipsey, 1981, pp. 45-48.] However, they differ in the borders they draw between them and in how they subdivide the categories.

Ginzburg [1965, p. 22] simply lists sixteen examples of private nonprofit enterprises by industry, from "mutual insurance companies" to "museums and libraries." His list is not intended as a classification scheme.

Oleck [1974, pp. 18-21] classifies private nonprofit enterprises by legal forms which correspond to those used for firms: individual enterprise (single proprietorship), association (partnership), and corporation (corporation). Two additional categories without profit-seeking counterparts are the foundation and the "corporation sole," a special type of one-person enterprise, e.g., a bishopric. He then devotes a separate chapter to "special organizations" classified by industry or broad type: agricultural organizations, labor unions, cooperative, etc.

Clarkson [1980] does not break down the category of private nonprofit enterprises, but he groups them with firms which are subject to price regulation or control into a category called "nonproprietary organizations" (see Chapter 4 below). Anthony and Herzlinger do not break down their category either, but they exclude mutual insurance companies and include proprietary hospitals as "nonprofit organizations," and they treat TVA as a "borderline case" [1980, pp. 32-33].

Hansmann [1980, pp. 884-890] distinguishes "nonprofit enterprises" from "limited-profit enterprises," which include regulated firms, limited-dividend companies (government-sponsored urban-development firms), cost-plus contracting firms, and cooperatives. He subdivides nonprofit enterprises in two ways [pp. 840-843]: by financing (donative versus commercial) and by control (mutual versus entrepreneural).

For our purposes as economists, a systematic classification into categories meaningful to us will be needed as we develop a "micro-micro" theory of organizations [Leibenstein, 1979]. The listing of organizations by industry does not serve our purposes in the study of firms.

The reason is suggested by Weisbrod [July 1978, p. 20, footnote reference omitted]:

> The published literature on models of nonprofit organizational behavior focuses on specific industries, primarily on models of hospitals, but also on schools or departments within schools. In our traditional theorizing about the behavior of private business firms we have, fortunately, not developed a distinct theory for the steel industry, another for the baking industry, and yet another for retail department stores. Similarly, in the nonprofit area we need more general, not industry-specific, models.

The same reasoning applies to classification by legal form.

Perhaps the best approach is to recognize three continua of organizational characteristics: ownership, control, and financing. This scheme combines the economist's basic types of organizations with Hansmann's two-dimensional classification.

Let us first separate out the one type of economic organization which exists for the basic purpose of consumption: the household. All other types of organizations exist for the purpose of production, broadly conceived, and can thus be called "enterprises." Thus the set of all nonprofit organizations includes households, by the definition in Chapter I, but the set of all nonprofit enterprises does not.

We can now apply our three-way scheme to the

enterprise.

The Ownership Dimension

Along the ownership continuum are three broad
categories: public nonprofit, private nonprofit, and
private profit. Public nonprofit enterprises are
called "governments," private profit enterprises are
called "firms," but there is no commonly accepted
synonym for "private nonprofit enterprises." (I suggested "charities" [Gassler, both 1979, 1980], but
it was not everywhere well-received.) Our own terminology, however, has the advantage of showing the
relation between our three-fold division and the
"public-private" and "profit-nonprofit" distinctions
we may also wish to make.

At the one extreme are the public nonprofit
enterprises. Two points which otherwise might cause
confusion should be made about them. First, any sub-
division of a government is a "bureau" by our usage
regardless of how independent it is from the legisla-
ture or executive (see Chapter IV). Thus, the Office
of Management and Budget, the Department of the Trea-
sury, the Federal Reserve System, and the National
Railroad Passenger Corporation are all bureaus of the
Federal Government, not independent organizations,
even though the latter two operate by law with a
large degree of autonomy. Second, there is thus by
definition no such thing as a "public profit enterprise." A government may choose to designate one of
its bureaus as a "profit center" [Anthony, 1980,
pp. 81-84], but the "profits" nonetheless accrue to
the government, not to any individual. (Note that
our term "public nonprofit enterprise" refers to an
entire government, and thus differs from the term
"public enterprise" in the industrial organization
literature [Turvey, 1971]. Shepherd calls these
"public corporations" [1979, p. 113], and Scherer
calls them "publicly owned enterprises" [1980,
pp. 486-490]. As long as we keep our definitions distinct, there are apparently more than enough terms
to go around.)

At the other end of the continuum are the private profit enterprises. The legal distinction between single proprietorships, partnerships, and corporations has generally not received more than a nod
in economics literature, as most of it concentrates
on the latter. However, some attention has been paid

to what Hansmann call "limited-profit" enterprises [pp. 884-890], the most important of which are regulated firms and cooperatives. There is some disagreement over whether these organizations should be considered profit or nonprofit. However, since they meet our simple definition of profit organization in Chapter I, they will be considered profit organizations here. Since the government regulates all types of organizations, there seems no compelling reason to shift a regulated firm to another category just because it is regulated. Cooperatives exist for the benefit of their members and distribute profits to certain of them, so they fit into the spirit of profit enterprises as a result. (For situations in which it is better to group cooperatives and regulated firms with nonprofit enterprises, Clarkson's "nonproprietary" term can still be used.)

Private nonprofit enterprises are distinguished negatively: they are different from governments in that they are not public, and they are different from firms in that they are not profit-oriented. Thus they can be seen as a middle category between the other two.

There are two additional categories of organizations which fit in the cracks between the main ones. Boulding calls organizations which straddle the public-private distinction or the profit-nonprofit distinction "intersects" [1973, p. 179]. Examples of organizations which straddle the public-private distinction would be the regional councils of governments or corporations of which a government may own part, and individuals or another government may own another part (e.g., The Port Authority of New York and New Jersey). The intersect organizations on the profit-nonprofit borderline include what can be called "income-seekers' nonprofit enterprises": e.g., trade associations, chambers of commerce, professional societies, labor unions, the New York Stock Exchange, the Committee for Economic Development, the Conference Board, and Business International. They do not themselves make profits, but they exist partly to increase the incomes of their member individuals or organizations.

The Control Dimension

The second continuum measures the degree to which the organization is subject to formal nonmarket

41

control by its beneficiaries [Hansmann, 1980, p. 841]. If control is absent or small, it is an "entrepreneural" organization; if present and large it is "mutual."

Public nonprofit enterprises could be divided into autocratic and democratic in this dimension, though that is a topic best explored within political science and public-choice theory. Public-private intersects include the Port Authority of New York and New Jersey (entrepreneural) and the Central Colorado Library System (mutual).

Private profit enterprises of the entrepreneural kind would include all single proprietorships, partnerships, and corporations. Cooperatives are mutual, however, whatever their kind. Consumers' cooperatives give formal nonmarket influence to demanders; producers' and workers' cooperatives give it to their suppliers. Similar arguments apply to employee-stock-ownership plans, employee-run corporations, etc.

The profit-nonprofit intersects seem to be mutual; it is difficult to imagine an entrepreneural organization helping others, but not itself, to make a profit. Trade associations, labor unions, and the like, are mutual organizations.

The distinction becomes most important in the case of the private nonprofit enterprises. The Educational Testing Service, the National Center for Higher Education Management Systems, Encyclopedia Britannica, CARE, the March of Dimes, The New York Public Library, Cooper Union, and the Roman Catholic Church are entrepreneural nonprofit enterprises. The American Automobile Association, Mutual of Omaha, the Great Lakes Colleges Association, Common Cause, United Way, the Friends Committee on National Legislation, and the American Historical Association are all mutual organizations.

The Financing Dimension

The third continuum is the financing dimension. At one end is the commercial enterprise which sells its output at or above its cost of production in a market. At the other end is the donative enterprise, which sells its output at a zero money price to one set of individuals, its "clients," and obtains its revenue from voluntary grants made by another set of individuals, its "donors." There is no necessary overlap between the set of clients and the set of donors.

Public nonprofit enterprises can of course co-erce individuals into being either donors (e.g., draftées, taxpayers) or clients (e.g., prisoners). They are donative in that sense universally, though they can choose to operate some of their bureaus on a noncoercive and even commercial basis.

Private profit enterprises are of course commer-cial by definition, except in special cases, e.g., government subsidies. Indeed, "solicitation of funds ordinarily may not be carried on without special authorization, which is implied by the state's accep-tance of a charter of a charitable corporation" [Oleck, 1974, p. 151], so firms are prohibited from asking for handouts from any outsiders except the government.

Private nonprofit enterprises and intersects of both kinds can be either commercial or donative. For the former, a further distinction could be made between "donative: nonendowed" and "donative: endow-ed." The spectrum now runs from those enterprises which obtain income tied directly to current produc-tion (voluntary hospitals, savings and loan associa-tions), to those which separate provision of services from receipt of donations in the current period (United Way, Democratic Party), to those whose pre-sent activities can be financed from donations receiv-ed in the more distant past (Cooper Union, Ford Foun-dation).

Table 1

Types of Economic Organizations

	Entrepreneural	Mutual
Public Nonprofit	USSR	United Kingdom
Intersects (Public–Private	Port Authority of NY and NJ	Central Colorado Library System
Private Nonprofit–		
– Commercial	Educational Testing Service Encyclopedia Britannica National Center for Higher Education Management Systems	American Automobile Association Mutual of Omaha TIAA–CREF
– Donative (Nonendowed)	CARE March of Dimes	United Way Common Cause
– Donative (Endowed)	New York Public Library Cooper Union Ford Foundation Roman Catholic Church	American Historical Association
Intersects (Profit–Nonprofit)	?	AFL–CIO U.S. Chamber of Commerce Committee for Economic Development
Private Profit	Single Proprietorships Goldman, Sachs & Co. Ford Motor Company	Cooperatives Lincoln Electric, Cleveland

Summary and Comments

The table shows the three dimensions together and indicates examples of each combination [American Historical Association, 1978, p. 79; Ginzburg, 1965, p. 22; Hansmann, 1980, p. 842; Oleck, 1974, Chapters 1, 42].

Clearly there is room for disagreement on detail. Hansmann [p. 842n] and Anthony [1980, p. 32] exclude mutual insurance companies from the nonprofit category, and the former specifically places them with the cooperatives. On the other hand, Oleck [p. 913] points out that cooperatives can be either profit or nonprofit.

However, the general outline of the classification, subject to refinement as research progresses, provides us with categories that are more or less operational and more or less easily applied objectively. As a consequence we can see certain patterns that can yield testable hypotheses. For example, we can expect commercial, entrepreneural, private nonprofit enterprises to operate very much like firms. We can expect donative, nonendowed mutual private nonprofit enterprises to be more likely to be engaged in redistribution in kind toward specific groups than to be involved in allocating quasi-public goods. The donative, endowed entrepreneural private nonprofit enterprises listed operate in areas with a much longer time horizon that their profit counterparts. These propositions are all subject to refinement and empirical verification.

Of course, organizations are not always what they seem. Private nonprofit enterprises are often operated by their managers as if they were "closet firms" (secretly profit-seeking) [Oleck, 1974, pp. 54-57]. Some private profit enterprises may acknowledge a "social responsibility" (e.g., Quaker entrepreneurs of the 19th century), thus operating at least partly as "closet private nonprofit enterprises. Regulation of firms by governments will tend to cause them to operate as "closet bureaus" of the government.

The extent to which an organization of one type will operate as a closet version of another type is a matter of degree. Sometimes it is difficult to tell whether the organization is acting as if it were a different type, or simply pursuing a conventional course in its own way. Is a firm which institutes a system of "consensus management" [Dowling, 1977] doing so because its managers feel a moral obligation to humanize the workplace, or because they believe it will increase profits? If the former is simply seen as a means to the latter [pp. 41-43], then the firm is acting as a firm. If the two are seen as separate goals and possible trade-offs are contemplated, then the firm is acting partly as a closet nonprofit enterprise.

Another example: suppose a farmer refuses to give up farming in spite of a long period of losses, subsidizing the activity with income from other sources. Is the farmer (a) operating the farm as a consumption good (i.e., for fun), (b) maximizing long-run profits over a long time span for the sake of children or grandchildren, or (c) acting as an irrational or excessively thickheaded "economic man"? If (a), the farm is part of the household, a glorified garden, not an enterprise. If (b), the farm is a firm but to some degree might be considered a nonprofit charitable enterprise, preserving its resources for future nonmarket redistribution. If (c), it is a firm, period.

The lesson of these comments is that it is better as a first approximation to avoid second-guessing in specific cases or groping for counterexamples. In creating a taxonomy to be of future use in developing theories of nonprofit enterprise, we should try to be as simple and straightforward as possible. To explain why nonprofit organizations of a given type are created, let us first as the question in general before attacking the particulars.

Goals and Objectives

We are now ready to take up the third of our five questions: "Why are nonprofit enterprises created?" It will be argued here that some of the goals and objectives of nonprofit organizations are the same as those of profit-oriented ones, and some differ. Within the organization the day-to-day motivations of the workers may often be similar throughout all types of organizations; the same may even be true of the founders to a lesser extent. The crucial distinction, however, is not in the day-to-day

operation of the organization but in the purposes
envisioned by the founders and expected by its pa-
trons and the public at large. Why am I pleased
when I see my stockbroker in a Mercedes, but a little
uncomfortable when I see a clergyman in the same
kind of car? Why do Anthony and Hirzlinger [1980,
p. 41] say about the performance of nonprofit enterprises:

> If managers who, based on experience
> in profit-oriented companies, are accus-
> tomed to the primacy of profits become
> involved in a nonprofit organization, they
> may find it difficult to adjust to their
> new environment and to relegate the finan-
> cial statements to the lesser status which
> they should have.

Chapter II provides clues to the answer to this question; we shall elaborate on it here.

First we shall discuss some characteristics
and problems of organizations in general. However,
our concern is not with the similarities between
profit and nonprofit enterprises, but with their
differences, so we leave a complete treatment of
that subject for other works. In the second section
we ask why anyone in an economy of rational individuals would choose to create or support a nonprofit
enterprise when a profit option exists. Neoclassical
economic theory, with its usual assumptions of individual selfishness and willingness to avoid free-
rider problems, can explain the creation of firms
and governments, but not of private nonprofit enterprises. In the third section we add the ingredients
for an explanation of why those organizations are
created.

There is one point which should be emphasized.
The discussion here is not about goods, but about
organizations. Many differences across sectors of
the economy can be explained, not by differences
in the goods themselves, but by differences in the
ownership characteristics of the organizations provid-
ing them. If economics has sometimes been called
the study of the behavior of commodities rather than
people, it has nevertheless had to make assumptions
about the actions of not only individuals, but organizations as well. However, it is true that the preoccupation with the behavior of prices and quantities

47

in market situations has, in the last few decades, caused the mainstream of neoclassical economic thought to take for granted many aspects of the relationship between individual preferences and organizational behavior. (The notable exception of the behavioral school makes its way into the textbooks only as a sidelight.) This is not to deny that there has been a payoff to the concern with externalities, interdependencies, and public goods. However, these are all properties related to commodities and only indirectly to group behavior through individual preferences.

Organizations in General

All organizations have some characteristics in common. Certain objectives and goals of the founders or the members of the organization may be the same whether it is a firm, a government, or a private nonprofit organization.

Kenneth Boulding has suggested that an organization may be a way of expressing some motive in its founder's personality. He suggest five such motives:

The first motive is self-perpetuation. The organization may be named for its founder, and the employees may hold the family name in a kind of reverent awe. A chief of state or government may see his or her other task as a means of entering the history books. The followers of a religious group may strive to build a large church or temple partly as an assertion of their own identity. The incumbent's image of the role of the office merges with the images of organization and self.

The second motive is self-protection, the avoidance of the risk of a threat to one's identity. The management of a foundation's endowment may follow a cautious investment policy and avoid dipping into its principal even in a crisis. Risk and uncertainty are a subject which is only now creeping toward the center of economic theory [Arrow, 1971, Chapter 6; Baumol, 1977, Chapters 17 and 25; Henderson, 1980, Chapters 3 and 5; Nicholson, 1978, Chapter 6].

The third motive is self-expansion. The Roman Catholic Church, the Communist Party, the Southern Baptist Convention, corporations, labor unions, and governments have felt motivated to expand their size and scope.

The fourth motive, self-challenge, is what motivates a gambler or mountaineer or an entrepreneur. A bank may keep a small business going during a depression on the gamble that the economy might some day come out of its collapse. A President of the United States may take draconian fiscal measures on the gamble that one curve will shift out just fast enough on the graph illustrating an untested economic theory.

These four motives build one upon the other in succession. The fifth one goes in the opposite direction: self-sacrifice. Some foundations and trusts may be established for a fixed period of time, to be abolished afterwards. The difficulty in coming up with examples of this type may be a testimony to their success.

Identity with organizations is bound up with a sense of dignity. Banks are known for their formal architecture and conservative style. Of course, dignity may be an effect of the motive for self-preservation: banks are required to show the need for their services and the probity of their owners in order to get a charter [Shepherd, 1979, p. 308].

Motives such as these may be operating in non-profit enterprises, but they operate in firms as well. They also seem to be as much related to means as to ends, to how an organization works rather than why it is created. Thus they fall under the jurisdiction of the general theory of organizational behavior rather than the special economic theory of non-profit enterprise developed here.

The same is true for the subject of decision-making processes and rules. It is agreed that individuals in organizations make decisions based on their images of the future, which are in turn based on information feedback from their environment. It is also agreed that they apply a valuation system to their agenda of possible futures to determine which they will attempt to realize.

What is controversial is the degree to which that decision-making process conforms to the economist's model of rational behavior, i.e., utility maximization. Herbert Simon [1976, 1979] and the rest of the "behavioral school" in economics have developed an alternative model of rational behavior based on "satisficing" rather than maximization. For our purposes here, however, the controversy is irrelevant for two reasons. First, the present study is an inquiry into the scope and limits of neoclassical economic theory in the study of nonprofit enterprise, and an attempt to modify and extend that role in several areas. Thus it is not within our scope to consider alternative schools within economics or elsewhere: behavioral, institutional, or, for that matter, symbolic-interactionist. Second, a major conclusion of Simon's work is that organizations of all types use efficiency as a basic criterion of choice [1976, pp. 118-122]. His criterion of efficiency is the same as that of the neoclassical economists [p. 39]; specifically, it conforms to the neoclassical notion of an expansion path. We come to essentially the same conclusion about the importance of efficiency in Chapter IV.

The literature of economics and of organizational behavior have also become concerned with the question of the relation between individual preferences and organizational goals. This problem is called the problem of "goal compatibility," "goal congruence" [Anthony, 1980, p. 18], "social choice" [Williamson, 1967, Chapter 8], or "group choice" [Meyer, 1976, Chapter 18]. There are a number of quite different approaches to this subject even within economics. X-efficiency theory [Leibenstein, 1966, 1979, 1980] focuses on the relation between the organization and its employees. The issue of separation of ownership from control [Berle, 1968] concerns the relation between the organization and what Simon [1976, p. 118] calls "the group that holds the legal control." The literature of public-choice theory is relevant to the question of how the members of the controlling group reach decisions; Arrow voting paradoxes can occur on boards of directors or trustees as well as in elections and legislatures:

> The management team of a nonprofit organization often will not agree on the relative importance of various objectives; members will view a proposal in terms of the relative importance that they personally attach to the several objectives of the organization [Anthony, 1980, p. 40].

50

Nonprofit Organizations

The third question can be restated bluntly: "Why would anyone in their right mind want to create a private nonprofit organization?" The phrase "in their right mind" to an economist means "behaving according to criteria of economic rationality." Why would a rational economic individual wish to create (or donate to) a nonprofit enterprise? Why would a society consisting entirely of such individuals create ownership and tax laws to permit and encourage such organizations? Neoclassical theory makes the rationality assumption, and nonprofit enterprises clearly exist, so the question must be answered.

Chapter II hinted at part of the answer: anyone interested in having an economic system in the first place would wish to see some enterprises perform the environmental and systemic functions, and anyone interested in seeing the economy function properly would wish to see enterprises performing the allocative, distributive, and stabilizational functions also. It is thus plausible that economically rational individuals may support the creation of nonprofit enterprises (and mechanisms to overcome free-rider problems if they appear).

Neoclassical theory, however, usually assumes not only economic rationality, but also selfishness. Can it still explain the existence of firms, governments, and private nonprofit enterprises?

Rationality, selfishness, and the absence of concern with free-rider problems are sufficient to explain an economic system which contains nothing but firms. Rationality, selfishness, and concern with free-rider problems in allocation can explain a system with both firms and governments; the latter would be sufficient to overcome free-rider problems with coercion.

If we relax the assumption of selfishness and allow benevolence [Hochman, 1969, 1970], we can allow the government to determine the distribution of income, which is otherwise subject to free-rider problems [Nicholson, 1978, pp. 666-668]. Actually, in free-rider situations, the distinction between selfishness and benevolence breaks down (see Chapter II). So where are the private nonprofit enterprises?

Private Nonprofit Enterprises

We are left with one other possibility: Unselfishness and absence of concern for free-rider problems. Once we allow for situations which meet this description, we find a niche for private nonprofit enterprises to fill.

"Unselfishness" is a broad category [Collard, 1978, Chapter 1; Dye, 1976, pp. 34-39]. Essentially it means that something other than a person's own consumption of goods and leisure enters into that person's utility. It can be someone else's private consumption or someone else's utility; if the relationship is positive, it is benevolence, if negative, malevolence. (Private nonprofit enterprises can be organized with malevolent goals: members of street gangs may be benevolent toward each other, but the group may have malevolent goals toward outsiders.) Alternatively, unselfishness can imply that the general state of the world (or some aspect of it) enters into utility. For example, the quantity of quality of some product not entirely produced or consumed by oneself might enter into one's utility. A nonprofit enterprise could thus be created from a concern for output rather than income. Indeed, if the interest were only in income, why not just start a firm?

Thus, we have an explanation for the creation of both governments and private nonprofit enterprises, one which fits in with Anthony and Hirzlinger's definition:

> A nonprofit organization is one whose goal is something other than earning a profit for its owners. Usually its goal is to provide services. [Anthony, 1980, p. 31.]

The subject of benevolence is further explored in the chapter appendix.

Conclusion

The answer to our third question can be provided by an expanded neoclassical model. Why do there exist firms, governments, and private nonprofit enterprises simultaneously? Because even though their employees may have the same types of motives from day-to-day, their founders have different types of goals. For firms, the goal is related to income, with no concern for a free-rider problem. For governments, the goals include concern for overcoming free-rider problems. For private nonprofit enterprise, the goal is related to output, with no (or less) concern for free-rider problems.

Constraints

The fourth question is: "How do nonprofit enterprises operate?" Here we interpret the question to mean: "What are the constraints under which nonprofit enterprises make choices?" Again, we find that some constraints are similar among all types of organizations, and some differ systematically among different types.

All organizations operate under production and social constraints. The former comprise the technological relationships between inputs and outputs, and the latter consist of the relationships among the organization's members. Leibenstein [1979] claims these constraints are inseparable from each other, but that does not affect our argument. For example, all organizations have some amount of benevolence among their members to facilitate ongoing work relationships not amenable to contracting, and to provide nonpecuniary compensation for employees. In fact, organizations in general operate with a mixture of selfish and benevolent relationships among their members [cf. Boulding, 1973].

Profit enterprises can afford a mixture that contains only a little benevolence and a preponderance of selfishness, since the profit criterion and exchange relationships insure (in a perfect world) compatibility between the organization's activities and the interests of the rest of society, and both profit and exchange operate on the selfish motives of individuals. The same is true for internal constraints, i.e., those imposed by the controlling group on the other members to induce their compliance with organizational goals.

Not so with nonprofit enterprise. Since their organizational goals are often partly or wholly connected with output, not income, they have strong elements of benevolence as a result. Too much

selfishness is an abuse of its purposes. Thus, there
develop constraints, both external and internal,
which are designed either to reduce the selfish components of the relationships between society, the
organization, and its members, or to make individual
selfish motives compatible with benevolent group
goals.

This section discusses the different types of
constraints that operate in private nonprofit enterprises. (Public choice theory and political science
concern themselves with the public ones.) The discussion is carried on under three headings: external
constraints, the target groups, and internal constraints.

External Constraints

External constraints are those which originate
outside the organization and influence its interaction with its physical and social environment.
Private nonprofit enterprises face constraints from
both the economic and the political institutions
in society. Constraints from the former are imposed
through the capital market; from the latter they
come through regulation and tax policy. Private
nonprofit enterprises have a different relationship
to the capital market from firms. They are sometimes able to borrow [Gross, 1979, pp. 342-343]
but due to the nonprofit constraint they are unable
to sell shares of stock. Instead, they can sometimes
solicit donations for their "endowment," which, like
equity capital, consists of funds that do not have
to be paid back. Unlike equity capital, however,
these funds are not always used for the purchase
of real capital; they are instead loaned out and
the enterprise uses only the interest. Of course,
many enterprises solicit donations directly tied
to the purchase of a particular piece of capital
(a new gym, an addition to the cathedral), but again
unlike the case of firms, these are gifts rather
than loans. Thus there are significant differences
between profit and nonprofit enterprises in their
relationship to the capital market. Whether these
differences put the nonprofit enterprises at a
advantage or disadvantage relative to firms is a
complicated question that awaits research on, among
other things, the relative effectiveness of stock
markets and equivalent grants processes in efficiently coordinating the interests of individuals and

54

enterprises.

One puzzling question along these lines is whether nonprofit enterprises are better able to grow
than firms:

> While nonprofit enterprises obtain
> capital from various sources, they need
> not contemplate paying dividends. . . .
> The direct financial return anticipated
> by an investor in a private [profit] enter-
> prise is not expected by donors to a non-
> profit organization [Ginzburg, 1965,
> pp. 73-74].

Thus, nonprofit enterprises have a built-in
fund for expansion, since their net revenue is 100%
retained earnings. A firm must plan to pay out some
minimum amount in dividends to keep stockholders
interested. So why are private nonprofit enterprises
not growing faster than firms? Why are the largest
organizations in the capitalist world mostly multinational corporations? Is it the relative strength
of selfishness over benevolence, diseconomies of
scale in labor-intensive service industries where
nonprofit enterprises concentrate, or some other
factor?

The political system also imposes constraints
on private nonprofit enterprises. Laws and regulations govern how they may be created, what activities
they may perform, what liability rules govern them,
how they organize meetings, relations between trustees and employees, what procedures they follow in
lawsuits, how they cope with bankruptcy, and how
they are abolished [Oleck, 1974].

Many regulations are designed to grant special
privileges to private nonprofit enterprises [Oleck,
1978, pp. 11-13; Ginzburg, pp. 68-70]. Lower postage
rates, exemptions from certain labor laws, exemption
from requirements to contribute to unemployment compensation funds, immunity from liability for negli-
gence, and licenses to solicit are examples.

Tax policy has been similar: most private nonprofit enterprises are exempt from Federal income
tax, state property taxes, and customs duties, and
contributions to nonprofit enterprises are deducti-
ble by donors.

According to Hansmann [1980, pp. 882-883], neither the exemption from the federal corporate income tax nor the exemptions from state and local real property taxes has been the determining factor in the expansion of private nonprofit enterprises. The most important reason is that the nonprofit enterprises predate the institution of the exemptions, and their expansion into new areas precedes the decisions to exempt those areas. The same is true on the other side for the charitable deduction [pp. 883-884], though Dye [1976] credits the contributions with having a high tax-price elasticity of demand.

However, tax policies influence the overall size of contributions to enterprises already established [Hansmann, 1980, p. 883; Dye, 1976]. This is not surprising; tax deductions clearly influence donors, not managers, and exemption of enterprises from taxes are a benefit that enterprises "pass on" to the donors: a donation of given size goes further because part of it is not siphoned off as taxes. Thus, tax policy influences decisions of donors to donate, but not decisions of founders to found.

What rationale governs the use of regulatory and tax policy to assist the "nonprofit sector"? Many of the activities which nonprofit enterprises perform have free-rider components which the government may attempt to offset; thus a balance is struck between the desire by the organization's founders to act through a private organization, and the desire by "society as a whole" to offset free-rider problems through public subsidy. There may also be the simple, vague notion that the economic system is tilted too far toward exchange, and that there needs to be a discretionary mechanism for correcting it.

Target Groups

The target groups consist of the organization's donors and clients. In the case of a firm, the two groups coincide exactly. In the case of a nonprofit organization, there is no necessary overlap between the two groups. A donative, nonendowed, private nonprofit enterprise such as CARE, for example, receives grants from one set of individuals to provide food to another set who may be halfway around the world [Hansmann, 1980, p. 847]. On the other hand, a commercial mutual private nonprofit enterprise such

as the American Automobile Association provides service to its members for an annual fee: the donors
and clients fuse into a single "membership" group.
The extreme example of separation of the two groups
might be in the case of the entrepreneural donative,
endowed, private nonprofit enterprise such as a foundation or charitable trust: the donor may be long
dead while clients are still receiving services.

It is unclear whether target groups should be
considered internal or external to the organization;
from the examples considered above it should be apparent that the question could be answered in different ways for different cases [Simon, 1976,
p. 113n].

The attitude of the controlling group and employees toward the target groups depends partly on
whether the organization is commercial or donative
[Anthony, 1980, pp. 43-45]. If commercial, the controlling group and employees are less likely to
perceive additional clients as a strain on resources;
their attitude will be less "bureaucratic." On the
other hand, if the organization is donative, it is
better able to pursue nonmarket goals, such as redistribution.

This point is tied in with the question of the
pricing of a nonprofit enterprise's services. Anthony
and Hirzlinger [1980, p. 380] state five principles
that should be thought through in deciding on a
price policy:

1. Services should be sold, rather than
   given away.
2. The price should affect the consumer's
   actions.
3. The price should ordinarily be equal
   to full cost.
4. The unit of service that is priced
   should be narrowly defined.
5. Prospective pricing is preferable to
   cost reimbursement.

These are not hard and fast rules; the authors point
out acceptable exceptions from each of them along
the way [Chapter 9]. For example, public goods
should not be sold; "subsidy" or "distributional"
pricing (at less than full cost) may be used if it
is decided to allocate services other than on an

ability-to-pay basis, and donations for operating
expenses may be deducted from costs in establishing
a price; the pricing unit should not be so defined
as to cause unnecessary paperwork; and for some projects (e.g., research and development) it may be
impossible to determine in advance how much they
will cost. The point is, however, that systemic
deviations from the principles should be carefully
established as policy, and if possible, costs should
be calculated and apportioned (and perhaps even an-
nounced) to each customer anyway.

The five principles and exceptions are really
a way of illustrating the trade-offs nonprofit enterprises face between the market-related goal of allocative efficiency and other economic goals, such
as distributive equity, merit-good provision, or
administrative simplicity (another kind of efficiency).

Internal Constraints

Since an organization consists of a set of individuals and network of formal and informal relationships between them, there will exist internal
constraints, i.e., relationships whereby one individual or group can alter the opportunities faced
by another. Many of these internal constraints will
be similar across organizational types: rules and
regulations, standard procedures, hiring and termi-
nation policies, relation of controlling group to
middle management, etc. However, there are significant differences as well, most of them stemming from
the difference in the role of profits in firms and
nonprofit enterprises:

> The absence of a satisfactory, single,
> overall measure of performance that is
> comparable to the profit measure is the
> most serious management control problem
> in a nonprofit organization. (It is in-
> correct to say that the absence of the
> profit _motive_ is the central problem; rath-
> er, it is the absence of the profit _mea-_
> _sure_.) [Anthony, 1980, p. 35, emphasis
> in original].

The consequences of this absence for nonprofit organizations are summarized by Anthony and Hirzlinger
[pp. 40-41]. First, there is no straightforward

way to aggregate and measure success in the achievement of multiple objectives (which nonprofit enterprises generally pursue). Second, there is no easy way to measure benefits of alternative courses of action. Third, there is no clear way to measure performance. Fourth, decisions must be more highly centralized rather than being left to the operating manager's discretion. Fifth, there is no easy way to compare the performance of different bureaus of the organization.

As a consequence, nonprofit enterprises face administrative problems which are often more difficult than those of firms. This is not always because the problems do not exist also for the latter, but because the profit measure cannot be used as an easy solution for the former.

The controlling group in most private nonprofit enterprises is a board of trustees or equivalent. In mutual enterprises, the controlling group is the entire membership, but the board may be the group which has the effective power most of the time. The board performs three essential functions. First, it initiates activities; in many cases the founders of the organization make up its controlling group. Second, it reviews and critiques proposals drawn up by the manager and staff. This is often done quite passively [Anthony, 1980, p. 47]. Third, it acts as the manager of last resort, taking over much closer supervision of the organization in a crisis. In the case of a mutual enterprise, the membership as a whole may get more involved. Citizens of a government, for example, may become closely involved in an election or revolution. The membership may also share responsibility with outsiders, for example, the government in the case of a regulated firm.

The functions are also performed by boards of directors in firms. However, in nonprofit enterprises,

> . . . There may not be a similarity between the objectives of the management and those of the [controlling] group that is close to the similarity that exists when both groups are essentially interested in profits [Anthony, 1980, p. 49].

This lack of goal compatibility thus might lead

boards to impose more constraints on the organization's other members than would a firm's board. This is not to say that the top management of the organization is motivated selfishly while only the board is interested in the organization's goal; on the contrary, top management may share those goals [Hansmann, 1980, Appendix]. However, no two people are likely to interpret or weigh those goals in exactly the same way.

The employees may also have evolved (or evolved from) a subculture of their own. The subculture of a university differs from that of a monastery (except for graduate students), and both differ from that of a mutual insurance company or trade union. This subculture may help to prevent any organization, profit or nonprofit, from changing too radically the nature of its services; we can expect conglomerates to form through merger more often than through spontaneous moves into unrelated markets by a single firm.

Subcultures, like unions, are of different types, however. They can be peculiar to a single organization or to an occupational group. If the latter, there may arise goal incongruities from another source: the possible conflicts between organizational goals and professional ethics. For one thing,

> Codes of professional ethics, which arise out of the principal-agent [i.e., client-professional] relation and afford protection to the principals, can also serve as a cloak for monopoly by the agents [Arrow, 1979, p. 506].

Professional ethics are as likely, however, to increase goal compatibility as decrease it, for example by strengthening preferences by professionals for rendering high-quality service in situations where clients are unable to judge quality easily for themselves. This may fit in well with the organization's nonprofit goals [cf. Hansmann, 1980, Appendix].

The accounting systems used in nonprofit enterprises in the U.S. differ from those used by firms in five significant ways [Gross, 1980, Chapter 2]. First, they often operate on a "cash" versus "accrual" basis, recording only transactions that have taken place, not obligations that have been incurred. Second, they often do not always record promises to pay; an account receivable is a legal obligation, but a pledge is not.

Third, nonprofit enterprises often must use "fund accounting," i.e., separate their accounts into categories corresponding to restrictions on their use: endowment, building, unrestricted, etc. Fourth, as a consequence, they may record transfers between funds and "appropriations" (setting aside part of a fund for a certain purpose).

Fifth, and perhaps most important, nonprofit enterprises do not always record their fixed assets. The balance sheet of the nonprofit enterprise looks very much like the balance sheet of a firm. The assets

> will include cash, bank deposits, securities of various kinds, accounts receivable, the quantities of all the kinds of goods, finished, in process, or raw, that it possesses, the quantities of all different kinds of buildings, land, machinery, etc. The accountant's balance sheet usually stops at this point, though occasionally an item for 'goodwill,' reflecting the value of the firm's market position, is included. In the economist's description there should perhaps be found some account of the firm's market position and also some account of its potential resources. [Boulding, 1950, p. 28.]

Goodwill is of great importance to many charities whether it shows up in their accounting systems or not: their mailing list of potential donors symbolizes the present value of their potential grants for operating expenses (and perhaps endowment).

Since nonprofit enterprises have such a reliable method of soliciting contributions that they could almost be considered private tax collectors, with shame (and maybe a little pressure from the foreman at work) as the enforcer instead of courts and police. The United Fund and churches with strong "stewardship" campaigns might come close to this.

Unfortunately, there is often no easy way to

record the assets of a nonprofit enterprise. Not all of them have such secure channels for their contributions. More importantly, the balance sheet does not easily account for intangibles. Assets are valuable according to the value of the things they can produce; net worth to a nonprofit enterprise is not as easy to calculate as it is for a firm: the former inescapably must refer to its net worth to society. Since so many of the outputs of nonprofit enterprises do not pass through markets in the same way that those of firms do, there is no clear way to assign an even approximate social value to them.

Boulding [1950] claims that the balance sheet is the fundamental determinant of the behavior of the firm [pp. 26-27]. However, the "true" balance sheet of the nonprofit enterprise cannot fully be known through its financial accounts. Thus we are not surprised by the fact that those accounts are given a lower status than they would be for firms.

Conclusion

We have answered our third and fourth questions. To the third question, "what do nonprofit enterprises do?," we answer that they pursue goals related to the reduction of free-rider problems and/or the production of output. They do, however, have greater potential for goal incongruity than do firms.

To the fourth question, "how do they operate?," our answer is that they operate under constraints which may differ from those faced by firms, because the lack of a profit measure make it otherwise more difficult to insure goal congruity.

This chapter as a whole asks the question: "What are nonprofit enterprises like?" Our answer is that they are just like firms, only different.

Appendix

Benevolence and the Theory of Individual Economic Behavior

The focus of this book is on nonprofit enterprises as organizations, but any theory of human organization must begin with assumptions about the behavior of individuals. In this and later chapters it is assumed that certain economic agents act benevolently, so a short discussion of economic benevolence is in order here.

The term "benevolence" is used here, instead of the more common term "altruism," for two reasons. First, it has an opposite, "malevolence," which the other term does not. Second, it is less ambiguous: many economists use the term "altruism" to refer also to feelings that are ultimately self-centered, a usage we specifically exclude below.

This appendix attempts to accomplish two tasks. The first task is to establish that "economic benevolence" is not a contradiction in terms, but is a subject worthy of serious study. The second task is to lay the groundwork for certain parts of the arguments made in later chapters. Most of the discussion here is based on Collard [1978, Chapters 2 and 12].

Benevolence vs. Selfishness: Alternative Views

A popular view of nonprofit enterprises in recent years, both within and outside the economics profession, has been what can be called the cynic's view. Keating and Keating assert [1980, p. 48]:

> Administrators in not-for-profit firms try to maximize, among other things, the gap between the funds that they actually need to perform the minimum level of service expected and the total size of the budget.

Alchian and Allen provide an elaboration of this view in their use of the Rose Festival Association of Pasadena, California, as a "textbook case" [1977, p. 117]:

> But someone has to set the ticket price. The person in charge could set a low price, so that more seats are demanded than are available. He might then, by virtue of his position, secure tickets and resell some at higher market-clearing prices, thereby unethically diverting wealth to himself. Being moral, he

certainly eschews <u>this</u> line of "gain"
-- and uses another. By underpricing the
tickets, he gets some for himself more
cheaply, releasing a bit of his own wealth
for other uses. Also, an excessive demand
for tickets permits him to favor some appli-
cants. The "right" people get tickets
at a price less than they <u>and others</u> are
willing to pay. In return, he is invited
to the best places and clubs; and when
he buys a car or furniture, past favors
are fondly and effectively recalled.

The cynic's view has to a large degree replaced
another view which was more popular in the past,
the Polyanna's view. That view said that since nonprofit enterprises existed for the betterment of
humanity and not for profit, they were therefore
exempt from much of economic analysis, and we could
therefore assume away any problems they had in helping society reach its collective optimum.

The Polyanna's view is less popular these days
and at its height was used mainly as a justification
for government economic activity, which is its use
today as well. No one -- including its strongest
supporters -- seems to take it seriously except as
a first approximation. Therefore it is not necessary
to discuss it at length.

The cynic's view, on the other hand, is taken
much more seriously by its followers. There are
at least two weaknesses in the basic argument itself
which are worth a bit of attention.

The first weakness is in the apparent circular-
ity of the whole argument itself. Starting with
the usual economic assumptions of individual selfishness and profit-maximization, the cynic tries to
demonstrate that the participants in nonprofit enterprises are acting out of selfishness and profit maximization. The line of reasoning is reminiscent of
the classical economist who argues that assuming
full employment, economic theory shows that involuntary unemployment is impossible, or of the contemporary economist who tries to show that, in a regime
of positive prices, "there is no such thing as a
free lunch."

The second weakness in the cynic's view is that

it begs the question of why nonprofit enterprises exist in the first place. Why would a selfish entrepreneur set up an organization as a nonprofit enterprise rather than a firm? (The discussion here is confined to nonprofit enterprises that perform a distributive function. Other functions performed by nonprofit enterprises are discussed in Chapter II.)

One answer that comes back is the tax laws. But why are the tax laws written to encourage nonprofit enterprises? Some say that it is because unscrupulous lawmakers want to deceive the gullible public into believing that nonprofit enterprises "do good," when they in fact do not. But then why would a selfish public care about "doing good"? If they were consciously selfish, they could not be gullible, and the sham would not be necessary. Others say the tax laws (and other laws) are the result of a complicated bargain between rich and poor classes. The poor think they are getting a lot and the rich think they are giving a little. But why would a bargain among selfish classes necessitate an organization other than a firm?

We are left with the conclusion that, for nonprofit enterprises to exist, <u>someone</u> in the society must think it is nice to be nice. As long as we believe that at least one individual is to some degree benevolent (and who of us would deny that for ourselves?), then it is only a small step to believing that people in general have benevolent as well as selfish motivations.

As a matter of fact, most economists seem to believe that people are capable of benevolent action on the individual level. Alchian and Allen themselves will be cited below as making that assertion; Hirshleifer's text contains several examples of this type of behavior [1980, pp. 81-83, 157-160, 545-546]. However, many economists fall back implicitly or explicitly onto a selfishness assumption when they look at individuals within organizations. They fail to remember Hirshleifer's own sharp words introducing his "positive" analysis of government:

It is sometimes thought that the difference between behavior in the marketplace and behavior in the political sphere lies in the realm of <u>motives</u>: self-

65

interest is expected to be the governing force in economic decisions, while in their political decisions people are supposedly concerned primarily with the public interest. This naive view is rejected here. The individuals who interact in their economic decisions are the same people, with the same motives, as those engaging in or subject to political decisions. To compare and contrast political and economic behavior we must look not to differences of motives but to differences in the <u>processes of human interaction</u> -- differences in the "rules of the game." [1980, p. 533, emphasis his.]

Benevolence and Selfishness: The Middle View

This chapter explores certain implications of the simple assumption that individuals are not always selfish, but they can sometimes display benevolent behavior toward each other or toward society as a whole. (Indeed one can make no stronger assumption than that people possess some benevolent as well as selfish motives without running into logical problems. [Collard, 1978, p. 9.]) Various forms of these benevolent feelings will be described and their consequences discussed.

The sources of these feelings, however, will not be discussed: we can think of them as arising from tradition, or from a selfish desire for status in this world or a good spot in the next. They can even arise from some sort of genetic self-interest in maximizing chromasomal survival [see Becker, September 1976, and Barash, 1977]. All these motives can have the same result: one person's pleasure depends on the pleasure or at least the consumption activity of another.

A succinct argument for introduction of benevolence into economic analysis is given by Alchian and Allen [1977, p. 118. For an extended argument, see Collard, 1978, pp. 4-5]:

The <u>economics</u> of charity or gifts may seem contradictory. How can people give gifts if they are assumed to be selfish? Selfishness, however, was not assumed (in this textbook): the postulates of

66

economic theory do <u>not</u> say that man is concerned only about himself. Each of us can be, and is, concerned about other people's situations.

Arrow [1974, in Phelps, 1975, p. 17] distinguishes three categories of benevolence:

(1) The welfare of each individual will depend both on his own satisfaction and on the satisfactions obtained by others. We have here in mind a positive relation, one of altruism rather than envy.

(2) The welfare of each individual depends not only on the utilities of himself and others but also on his contributions to the utilities of others.

(3) Each individual is, in some ultimate sense, motivated by purely egoistic satisfaction derived from the goods accruing to him, but there is an implicit social contract such that each performs duties for the other in a way calculated to enhance the satisfaction of all.

The present book excludes (3), leaving it for now to the public-choice economists. Actually, (3) is a special case of what Boulding [1973] calls "reciprocity," which is a type of intertemporal exchange at fuzzy terms of trade. If I do something nice for you now because I think you may do something nice for me in the future, that is reciprocity. If I do something nice for you and expect nothing in return, that is benevolence ("For greater love . . ."). Kurz in two papers on altruism [1977, 1978] is discussing reciprocity, not benevolence: in the 1978 paper he says, "in an altruistic equilibrium all individuals act altruistically since it is in their individualistic best interest to act that way." The strategic behavior described by Schelling in his short 1978 <u>AER</u> article is merely an elaboration of the selfishness theme.

The point of view taken here is a difficult one to take, as are many middle-ground positions. The attempt will be to incorporate both the selfish and the benevolent motives into a model of individual economic behavior. (A perfectly general theory would

have to include at least two other motives: pure
malevolence, which is more or less the opposite of
altruism, and combined motives, such as those which
cause a parent to punish a child "for your own good"
or a voter to favor taxation for a new public project. [See Boulding, 1973, p. 34.]) As it turns
out, this will involve not only the trade-off between
own consumption and consumption by others, but also,
as we shall see later, trade-offs between own leisure
(or other reserved input) and production of a good
for another.

Evidence for Benevolence

Most economists are not used to looking for
evidence of benevolence, but some have recently decided that there is a lot of it going around. Phelps
[1975, p. 2] writes:

> The range of altruistic behavior,
> in what we commonly interpret as such,
> is impressive. It is sometimes exhibited
> (for good or ill) by buyers and sellers
> in the marketplace. The presence of altru-
> istic behavior, as economic behavior in
> general, is even more pronounced away from
> commercial settings. More than half of
> the American population depend for their
> security and material satisfactions not
> upon the sale of their services but rather
> upon their relationships to others.

Kenneth Arrow [1974, in Phelps, 1975, pp. 16-17]
reports on the findings of Richard Titmuss in his
comparative study of provision of blood for trans-
fusions [1971]:

> A rough impression of the fragmentary
> United States data together with that for
> the United Kingdom suggests that unpaid
> donations are distributed among socio-
> economic classes more or less in proportion
> to the relative size of each class. Paid
> donors, on the contrary, are drawn almost
> exclusively from the lower-income categor-
> ies, including the unemployed.

So benevolence, at least with respect to blood donations, is distributed evenly among social classes.
If one bought the claim that the value of time is

higher for those with higher incomes, then one could argue that the even distribution indicates that the wealthy are more benevolent than the poor (i.e., that benevolence is a superior good). However, in the U.S. at least, there are enough rigidities and lumps in the labor market (fixed hours per week, etc.) and enough blood drives during working hours to weaken this argument considerably.

Notice that, as economists, we are not concerned with "how much" benevolence there is compared with "how much" selfishness. We are concerned with the questions: if benevolence exists at all, what affects it, what does it affect, and how is it related to the economy as a whole? Arrow confuses things a bit when he says [1974, in Phelps, 1975, p. 17]:

> Even in the United Kingdom [where all blood donations are unpaid] the percentage of the eligible population that gives blood is actually very small, only six percent according to Titmuss's estimates. Titmuss does not comment on this fact. The picture of a broadly altruistic society seems somewhat blurred when we realize what a small fraction of the population is in fact functioning altruistically.

Not at all. To find the scope of benevolence in an economy, one has to look at all benevolent activities, not simply those in one "industry." One could as well ask whether the fact that there are so few diamond dealers in the U.S. and U.K. (what percentage of the population?) means that people are not motivated very much by self-interest and profit.

Individual Welfare

In order to discuss benevolence more precisely, additional terminology is required. Collard [p. 18] distinguishes an individual's "private preferences" and "social preferences." Let us postulate the existence of an "individual welfare function" which would incorporate both selfish and benevolent motives. (A more general formulation would also include malevolent, or even combined, motives.) That term will be used here, and different formulations of the individual welfare function will be discussed.

69

Let

$$U_1(q_{i1},\ldots,q_{im})$$

be the <u>individual (selfish) utility function</u> of person i, defined over m attributable commodities. An attributable commodity [Collard, 1978, pp. 7-8] is one of which the consumption by each individual can be separated from that by any other individual. "Public goods" are non-attributable commodities. Collard [p. 8] points out that for non-attributable goods, the distinction between selfish and benevolent motives is blurred. We assume attributability for simplicity and will relax that assumption in later chapters.

We then define two types of individual welfare functions for person i, following Collard [pp. 7-8]. The first is the <u>utility-related individual-welfare function</u>.

$$W_1(U_1(q_{11},\ldots,q_{1m}),\ldots,U_1(q_{i1},\ldots,q_{im}),\ldots,U_n(q_{ni},\ldots,q_{nm})),$$

defined over the utilities of all individuals including the ith. The difference between

$$W_1 \text{ and } U_1 \text{ is that } U_1$$

captures the person's purely selfish motives, but

$$W_1$$

includes not only selfish but benevolent, envious, and other higher (or lower) motives in what Edgeworth [1881, p. 103] calls a "cool moment." In practice, some sort of average income distribution to various classifications of other persons might be a more realistic representation, or one such as Alchian and Allen describe [1977, pp. 118-119, emphasis theirs]:

> I would prefer other people to be richer than poorer, even if it costs me something. I would give them a dollar if my personal use of it meant less to me than would its increase of their wealth -- in <u>my</u> assessment of a most preferred situation. The larger my wealth relative to the poor, the greater my willingness to contribute to the poor, just as a larger

amount of candy increases my willingness to give up candy for cokes. This implies the richer contribute more to the poor; and they do. Furthermore, "matching grants" would induce me to give still more, because each dollar I give up gets more than a dollar to the poor. This implies that matching grants would be commonly observed in charity; and they are.

Collard [p. 9] refers to what he calls the "after-you problem," which applies to behavior motivated by functions of this type. If everyone were interested in giving all others what they want, no one would have decided what the "others" want, and the solution is indeterminate. A high school teacher in central Texas was fond of saying, "we are all here for a purpose, and that purpose is to help others." Help others do what? To avoid this problem Collard assumes that

$$\frac{\partial W_i}{\partial U_j} < 1, \quad i \neq j.$$

In other words, we do not love our neighbors as ourselves; at the margin we love them less.

An important advantage of this type of individual-welfare function is that it is subject to what Collard calls the "non-twisting theorem" [pp. 12-13, 21]. This says that, if individual-welfare functions for all individuals are of the utility-related type, "then the conditions for efficient exchange are precisely those in the selfish case." This implies that competitive equilibrium is sufficient to achieve an optimum and alternatives to the market are not necessary [pp. 12-13].

The most obvious disadvantage of this type of function is that it assumes the measurability by each individual of everyone else's utility functions. Not only does this require people to be able to do what economists have claimed for decades to be themselves unable to do, it also requires each individual to be able to tell the difference between other people's utility (which is what enters into the individual-welfare function) and their individual welfare (which is what is revealed by their

behavior). The measurability assumptions are com-
pounded.

Kenneth Boulding could have this type of function in mind when he says [1973, p. 12]:

> The willingness to make grants, in-
> deed, depends on two main factors: one,
> the perception of the efficiency of the
> grant; and the other, the degree of identi-
> fication with the welfare of the recipient,
> that is, the degree of benevolence. . .

(His definition of efficiency [p. 11] differs from
ours.) In our notation, the first factor is

$$\frac{\partial U_j}{\partial q_{ik}} \quad \text{and the second is} \quad \frac{\partial W_i}{\partial U_j}.$$

The second type of function is the <u>commodity-
related individual-welfare function</u> for individual
i:

$$V_i(q_{11},\ldots,q_{1m},\ldots,q_{i1},\ldots,q_{im},\ldots,q_{n1},\ldots,q_{nm})$$

which is defined directly over the allocations of
each commodity to each individual, including the
ith. Again, some sort of averaging and aggregating
might be more realistic, but here we assume preci-
sion.

A disadvantage of this formulation is that by
leaving out everyone's utility functions, it may
seem to imply a disregard for other people's happiness, which is the opposite of what we think of as
benevolence. It is this property which leads Collard
and others to label this "meddlesome" or "paternalistic." However, if it is impossible for a benevolent individual to measure other people's happiness,
then the next-best solution may be to measure their
consumption and take a guess as to what relation
it has to their utility. If the morally preferred
formulation is impossible, then we should be slow
to condemn the one that is left.

The more important characteristic of this function is that it is subject to the "twisting theorem"
[Collard, 1978, pp. 124-125]. Pareto-optimal

allocations in an economy of commodity-related individual-welfare maximizers bear no particular relationship to those that would exist if the individuals were all selfish. Therefore competitive equilibrium does not imply Pareto optimality, and other mechanisms have to be devised for reaching a Pareto-optimal solution.

Collard points out that the commodity-related (paternalistic) formulation has realism to recommend it [1978, p. 122]:

> The overwhelming weight of impressionistic evidence is that people are concerned less with other people's incomes or utilities than with their consumption of specific commodities. Any reader who believes himself to be entirely nonpaternalistic in his concern is asked to perform the folowing mental experiment: I notice that my neighbor is badly fed and badly clothed so I give him some money which he then spends on beer and tobacco. Do I feel entirely happy about this or do I somehow feel that my intentions have been thwarted?

Collard goes on [p. 123] to provide more quantitative evidence, citing Hochman and Rodgers' 1970 estimates that the percentage of redistribution "that seems to be made up of transfers in kind" are 42 in the United States and 50 in the United Kingdom.

Benevolence and Professionalism

So far benevolence has been discussed as though it had to do only with attitudes toward redistribution of income in kind or in cash. It might also be useful to see it in more general terms. If concern for society as a whole is really what benevolence is about, then it could include feelings about the legal and socio-political framework of the economy and the quality of work done whether or not the work is rewarded "properly" in the marketplace.

It is not difficult, for example, to see "professionalism" as a type of benevolence toward society in general and clients in particular. For example, professionals place greater value than others on building trust between supplier and demander. This helps to overcome the problem that supplier and

73

demander differ greatly in the degree of information they possess: The professional is often taught that it is part of his or her role to attempt as much as possible to follow the interests of the client, sometimes when the client may not even know what those interests are.

CHAPTER IV

A MODEL OF THE PRIVATE
NONPROFIT ENTERPRISE

Introduction

Even though the category "private nonprofit enterprise" includes a great many different kinds of organizations, we shall attempt to construct a general model to encompass all of them. In the first section we shall outline some of the approaches to the theory of the private nonprofit enterprise which have been developed in the past, then we shall describe an approach based on constrained maximization of managerial utility ("managerial welfare" in the language of the Appendix to Chapter III). The basic question addressed by our model is: does nonprofit status by itself necessarily imply inefficient purchase of inputs?

Economic Analysis and the Study of Private Nonprofit Enterprise

Economic theory has historically paid scant attention to nonprofit enterprises; consequently there are only a few formal models of their behavior. This section is devoted to a summary of several of those attempts to model such organizations in a mode which resembles the managerial-discretion approach developed by Oliver Williamson in his theory of the firm. A discussion of Williamson's approach is followed by reviews of models proposed by Joseph Newhouse, Estelle James, David Garvin, Kenneth Clarkson, and Dennis R. Young.

Williamson

Williamson's 1967 study reviews several "alternative" theories of the firm, formulates a managerial discretion model of its own for imperfectly-competitive firms, shows that it holds up under some empirical tests, and extends it is a later chapter to include group-choice considerations within the firm.

The "immediate determinants" of managerial behavior in Williamson's view are salary, security, "dominance" (status, power, prestige), social

service, and professional excellence. He proposes
a general model of "expense preference," the tendency for managers to favor certain categories of
expenditures over others, and he collapses the list
of motives into two categories of expense: staff
expenditures (salary, dominance, and partly, security
and professional excellence) and "emoluments," i.e.,
benefits such as expense accounts which must be used
at work and not at home (status, prestige).

The formal model takes expense preference to
mean the utility function of the manager and staff,
and emoluments to be arguments of that function.
A third argument, "discretionary profits," is added;
these are defined as profits earned over and above
the minimum amount necessary to keep the stockholders
from taking their money elsewhere. (Growth of the
firm is seen not as the end in itself, but as a means
to the attainment of these other goals [p. 30].
Robin Marris's model based on growth maximization
was published at the same time as Williamson's work
[Marris, 1963, 1964], and is not cited by him.)

Williamson [p. 32] argues that monopoly may
affect managerial goals favorably, an argument that
applies a fortiori to nonprofit enterprise:

> In terms of Maslow's hierarch of needs
> -- physiological, safety, love, esteem,
> and self-actualization -- . . . Maslow
> argues that higher order needs become acti-
> vated only when the lower needs are satis-
> fied. . . . In general, managers operat-
> ing firms in the monopolistic sector should
> have relatively more opportunity to become
> sated with respect to security and domi-
> nance needs [i.e., safety, love, and es-
> teem] and, hence, give more attention to
> professional objectives than would managers
> in the competitive sector. Indeed, social
> service objectives may even become opera-
> tive in regulated industries . . .

There are sound reasons for using the managerial-
discretion approach for many, if not most, firms.
However, for our study of nonprofit enterprises the
reasons for taking this path are even more compelling: nonprofit enterprises are constrained by law
not to distribute profits to anyone, therefore it
is awkward to conceive of them attempting to

maximize something that their members cannot have.

This is not to disagree with Weisbrod [July 1970, p. 20]:

> I do not dismiss the argument that many "nonprofit" organizations are actually profit-maximizers in disguise; some may simply pay above-market salaries to managers who are, in effect, receiving profits. Indeed, I believe the argument applies widely, as the very least to organizations that provide no significant amount of collective-goods outputs and receive essentially no contributions or gifts.

> What is in doubt, however, is whether a profit-maximization model also applies to those nonprofit organizations that are heavily dependent on donations and that provide largely collective-type goods and services.

The present chapter ignores those cases in which a private nonprofit enterprise may best be seen as a closet firm, without accepting Weisbrod's criteria for distinguishing them from the other case. Actually to some writers the operation of a nonprofit enterprise as a closet profit maximizer is seen as an abberation [Clarkson, 1980, pp. 17-18; Etzioni, 1976].

Much of the following analysis resembles the Williamson approach. Not only does it focus on managerial preferences and opportunities, but it also in general attempts to capture, within a conventional economic model, some ideas about private nonprofit enterprises which have so far mostly been explored verbally or from other perspectives [Garvin, 1980, Chapter 1].

This section adapts the Williamson formulation into a managerial utility model of a nonprofit enterprise, and it derives equilibrium properties for its behavior in input markets. Salary is included as a constraint and emoluments are included as "amenities" in the maximand. Security and status are ignored; power is assumed away since the manager is at the top of the organization. Prestige, social service, and professional excellence are captured by including output in the objective function. (Williamson eliminates social service in his analysis for simplicity; we keep it here for obvious reasons.) Group-choice considerations are ignored, and the enterprise is assumed to operate in perfectly-competitive input markets.

James

Estelle James (n.d.) applies a managerial-utility approach to private nonprofit enterprises (she calls them "nonprofit organizations," or NPO's): "their objective is to maximize utility subject to a zero-profit constraint."

In the James model, managerial utility is a function of quantity, price, and quality of output. (She ignores group-choice problems.) The implication she draws is that "competitive" NPOs in the short run produce more output than would competitive firms at the given market price. Her "competitive" NPO, however, faces a downward-sloping demand curve because "average fixed revenues" (e.g., gifts and subsidies) are added to the parametric price to get average revenue. Thus the "competitive" NPO behaves like a monopolistically-competitive firm.

The monopolistic NPO, able to choose both price and quantity of output, will charge a lower price than a monopoly firm, but it may produce a greater or lesser quantity. The argument depends on the assumption that price enters into the managerial utility function directly (with a negative derivative).

James discusses two reasons why NPOs might choose a different mix of inputs from what a perfectly-competitive firm would employ. First, managerial preferences may include specific inputs as well as output. Here James seems to imply that "the use of lavish expense accounts, plush offices, attractive secretaries, etc." [p. 7] are part of the production process. However, it would be better to consider only those inputs necessary for the production of a specific output level as arguments in the production function and to consider any "amenities" over and above that to be separate from production, but added into cost. This is implied in Williamson's formulations [1967, Chapter 4]. Theoretically it must be emphasized that there are two

78

distinct phenomena: an "inefficient" producer is distinct from an organization which produces output efficiently and also efficiently purchases amenities for its staff.

The second reason James mentions that NPO output would differ from competitive-firm output is that the legal status of NPOs allows them to be exempt from certain payments which lower their cost curves. She mentions volunteer labor as one of these exemptions, but that has nothing to do with the legal status of the NPO, nor does it artificially lower its cost curve. Volunteers could conceivably work for firms (though there are minimum-wage laws in many cases). The main point, though, is that volunteer labor is labor offered at a zero wage rate. There is nothing artificial about the lowered cost curve if it includes the fact that the labor market for certain employees has cleared at zero.

James makes a contrast between "pure production" activities and "pure consumption" activities of the NPO and mixtures between the types. Without going into detail, we can summarize the distinction by saying that the production activities, done at a "profit," subsidize the consumption activities, produced at a loss (excluding the utility they provide).

James correctly emphasizes the roles of "fixed revenues" in altering the behavior of NPOs from what a firm would do. However, though revenues are fixed with respect to output, they are not fixed with respect to everything: they vary with fundraising effort.

The present study excludes price from the maximand but includes output. Amenities are separated from the production function, and no distinction is made between "production" and "consumption" activities, since all production of output is assumed to be done for the purpose (_inter alia_) of satisfying someone else's wants even if it also satisfies the manager's. However, James' interpretation could conceivably be imposed on the model presented here. The concept of "fixed revenue" is also used, as a function of fundraising effort.

Newhouse

Joseph Newhouse's 1970 model of the nonprofit

hospital is by now well-known. The hospital decision-maker is assumed to maximize a function which includes quantity and quality of output as separate variables. (Group-choice problems are assumed away.) The hospital budget is the constraint.

Quality is measured by using cost as a proxy. Newhouse does not, however, use price as a separate variable: since the enterprise is faced by a downward-sloping demand curve, the presence of quantity in the maximand causes the decision-maker to keep price down. Newhouse mentions the possibility of fundraising by the hospital to cover its deficits, but he does not carry the notion very far.

The implications are that the hospital purchases its inputs inefficiently and does not set its output optimally. The implications result from the fact that the competitive forces operating in a perfect market with firms are weaker here due to the lack of a profit motive and the possible presence of barriers to entry by firms. The second implication also results from the existence of a quantity-quality trade-off which firms do not have and the possible biases toward quality by decision-makers in nonprofit enterprises.

This chapter does not include quality as a separate variable, since different qualities of the same product can simply be treated as different outputs or as multiples of a given quality; these are the ways quality is treated elsewhere in neoclassical economics. We do however exclude price from the objective function for reasons similar to his, and we carry the fundraising question farther along.

Garvin

David Garvin's study of universities [1980] uses a model similar to Williamson's. He assumes that the university acts as a single unit to maximize a utility function which depends on institutional prestige and quality and quantity of students. Institutional prestige is dependent on the prestige of the different academic departments, which in turn are functions of faculty quantity and quality. Student quality is a decreasing function of student quantity and an increasing function of institutional prestige. The budget constraint requires that revenues equal costs. Revenues come from tuition,

research, and outside aid for students. Costs are
the sum of the costs of acquiring faculty members
and the nonfaculty costs of educating students.

The Lagrangian and first-order conditions are
complicated, but the latter can be interpreted in
the usual way as marginal rates of substitution and
of transformation, taking all the interactions between variables into account. The effect is to show
"how universities balance the quantity and quality
of enrollments in determining the size and composi-
tion of their student bodies," and to show how
"increases in the number and quality of faculty members may have quite different effects on departments
in different disciplines" [p. 34].

Garvin addresses several criticisms that might
be levelled against this approach, arguing that alternative objectives are less satisfactory than utility maximization. In addition to explicitly rejecting
the hypothesis that universities maximize profits
(even though they are nonprofit), he rejects the
view that they maximize revenues as inconsistant
with the facts. Like Williamson he devotes an entire
chapter to the group-choice problem within the organization, attempting to demonstrate that the utility-
maximization assumption is plausible for an enterprise as complex as a university.

The present chapter adopts the same approach
toward the organization's maximand: it is a single
utility function, abstracting from internal decision-
making (group-choice) problems. It also adopts the
same type of zero-profit constraint. However, we
include output explicitly in the objective function
of the organization.

Clarkson

In a recent article published in the proceedings
of a conference, Kenneth Clarkson [1980] stresses
the importance of the differences in constraints
on managerial choices between "proprietary" and "nonproprietary" organizations, rather than differences
in the objectives they pursue. In both cases he
assumes the manager acts so as to maximize a utility
function of the usual shape.

Clarkson's definition of "nonproprietary" is
broader than our notion of "nonprofit." It includes,

for example, regulated firms and firms subject to government price controls. However, his focus is clearly on the organizations that meet our definition.

The variables in the manager's utility function are of two types: "customer outputs" and "employee outputs." The former are goods produced by the enterprise in question or by other enterprises and sold to outsiders (or to the manager acting as one), and the latter are the amenities of the job (fringe benefits, congeniality of other workers, etc.).

The differences appear in the budget constraint affecting the manager. In the case of a proprietary organization, the constraint includes the manager's share of the wealth (profits) of the organization, the manager's own wealth, and his or her purchases of customer and employee outputs from the enterprise itelf and of other customer goods from elsewhere. In the case of a nonproprietary organization the manager faces a zero-profit constraint and restrictions on the prices and quantities of customer and employee outputs.

Clarkson argues that many hypotheses concerning the differences in the behavior of nonproprietary as opposed to proprietary organizations can be explained in terms of the differences in the constraints on the manager's behavior imposed both within the organization (by stockholders or trustees) and outside the organization (by laws and government regulations). In addition, monitoring costs and procedures are important. If, and only if, these constraints and costs are specified in a particular situation we can say with certainty how the manager will behave -- for example, whether the manager of a nonproprietary organization will purchase more of a given input, or produce an output more expensively, or respond more quickly to a new opportunity, than the manager of a proprietary organization. The group-choice problem is sidestepped by assuming a single manager reports to a board of directors or trustees who set constraints; the focus is on the manager rather than the board.

Clarkson makes mention of the possibility that the outputs of nonproprietary oranizations may possess "invisible" attributes, i.e., attributes that cannot be monitored. He quotes Lindsay [1976,

p. 1068] as claiming that if such attributes exist in government enterprises, then average cost would be lower for government than for proprietary enterprises producing the same product.

The approach followed in this chapter closely resembles Clarkson's. The managerial utility function is defined over (customer) output and amenities, and the zero-profit constraint and manager's personal-income constraint resemble his. There is one major difference, however. Clarkson assumes the trustees act to minimize costs; we do not. In fact, that is precisely the question this chapter asks: "Does nonprofitness necessarily imply that a nonprofit organization will fail to minimize cost?" The contrast between Clarkson's article and this chapter is not as strong as it might first appear; it turns out to be more a difference of emphasis than of approach.

Young

Dennis R. Young [1983] asks the question, "If entrepreneurs are not allowed to keep the profits in a nonprofit organization, why would there be entrepreneurs in the nonprofit sector at all?" He identifies a dozen different types of entrepreneurs based on their motivation. Table 2 reproduces the table in his chapter 5, with the type of entrepreneur matched with motivation. Young then goes on to discuss the ways in which industries screen potential entrepreneurs by discipline (the health industry requires a medical or related degree for entry, and so on), and in which entrepreneurs and potential entrepreneurs sort themselves by industry according to the probability that a particular industry can provide opportunities to fulfill one type of goal or another. The same occurs by sector, i.e., in the screening by type of organization, profit or nonprofit, within each industry. Conditions such as the age of the industry or sector within the industry (how long have there been proprietary hospitals?) are important in this sorting process.

It is tempting to try a further categorization. Power and income seekers seem the most purely "selfish" of the lot; economists not only are not surprised to see them in the profit-making and government sectors, but we also usually assert that they are the only ones there, by assumption. Their utility functions are well-defined, and we have seen them before. Searchers seem to be a more interesting type of "selfish" entrepreneur, but still oriented on their own consumption or activities as a means to their own happiness. They may still be in the process of defining their utility functions, and we economists wait (analytically) until they are done before we incorporate them into our theory. Independents and conservers are oriented on the organization in which they may find themselves, and one might expect to find them in any organization regardless of sector. The economics of nonpecuniary benefits applies to them, and our model below includes "amenities," as we said before.

Table 2

Young's Entrepreneural Stereotype Models
[Table 5-1, p. 67]

Artist
    Architect   Pride in building and workmanship
    Poet   Creativity and implementation of ideas
Professional   Acclaim of disciplinary peers
Believer   Pursuit of a cause or mission
Searcher   Self-identity
Independent   Autonomy
Conserver   Preservation of a cherished organization

Power Seeker
    Controller   Stimulation and security of feeling in
                     control of people
    Player   Acclaim, notoriety, and excitement of
                     having power

Income Seeker   Wealth

Professionals and artists are oriented on the work they do; their utility derives from something that other people also notice and from which others may also benefit. Their utility functions include, at the very least, the utility of the output they produce, as well as the disutility of the work they do. (I do not enjoy rehearsing for hours at a time, but the satisfaction of knowing that I have directed a major musical event makes it all worthwhile.) The believer has perhaps the quintessentially benevolent motivation: the advancement of a cause greater than the self. (Presumably it could be a hostile motivation as well, or instead, but that is not the type that Young has in mind.)

These last three types, then, pose more of a problem than the others. It is difficult to predict the consequences of their behavior as entrepreneurs without incorporating their motivations into our analysis. The easiest way to do this is to include the output of their work in the utility function along with the work itself. This is what we do in what follows. Young takes his analysis in a less abstract dimension and so might claim that much is glossed over in our method, but for our purposes it captures an essential difference between the types of entrepreneurs we are used to seeing in firms, and those we can expect to see more often in the nonprofit sector.

A Simple Model

The following is a modification and extension of the models discussed above. Some of the implications of this model differ from those of the others in interesting ways.

Objective

We assume the private nonprofit enterprise is headed by a single manager who acts as if to maximize a utility function which possesses the usual properties of concavity and differentiability. (These assumptions can of course be modified without loss of generality to become simply strict quasi-concavity [Baumol, 1977, p. 233].) There are of course no group-choice problems in this formulation.

McGill and Wooten [1974, pp. 444-445] point out that nonprofit enterprises often suffer from "goal ambiguity." By assuming a single well-defined utility function we can assume that goal ambiguity has been resolved by including each goal as a separate output.

What arguments are included in the utility function? There are two contrasting views. Williamson [1967, p. 55] is not referring to nonprofit enterprises, but his words can be used as a summary of one view:

> . . . where discretion in the decision-
making unit exists, this will ordinarily
be exercised in a fashion that reflects
the individual interests of the decision-
makers.

The contrasting view is stated rather apologetically
by Newhouse [1970, p. 71]:

> Perhaps it is not too wide of the
mark to suggest that the chance to provide
a service will lead some altruistic citizens to try to establish a hospital. This
does not appear to be such a farfetched
explanation for the founding of either
hospitals or private colleges.

The first view argues for the inclusion of a variable
for "amenities." Amenities are items of personal
consumption which must be consumed on the job and
cannot be taken home: large desks, gold plated
curbs, and expense accounts. The second view argues
for incorporating the services performed by the enterprise. This assumes that the manager, if not one
of the founding donors, at least shares their motivations to some extent. (Perhaps the manager has sacri-
ficed a higher salary offered in the profit sector
[Hansmann, 1981, p. 889].) We include both. (In
the terminology of the Appendix to Chapter III, we
now have a "commodity-related individual-welfare
function," but we preserve the usual term "utility"
here for simplicity.)

Price is excluded from the maximand for the
reason given by Newhouse. Money income earned by
the manager (i.e., salary) should properly be considered in the constraints, and consumption and labor
should be the relevant arguments of the utility function. (Managers do not eat money, and we do not
here care about Pigouvian money balances.)

For reasons given earlier, quality is assumed
incorporated into the output variable and is not
given a status separate from the object of which
it is an attribute.

Thus the objective is:

$$(1) \quad \max \quad U[q_c, q_n, q_a, q_o]$$

where

$$q_c$$

is personal consumption (i.e., things "taken home" in the manager's role as consumer),

q_n is labor supply, q_a is amenities, and q_o is the output of the charity. Though we write them as scalars, they are assumed to be vectors; there are at least two goods consumed, at least two amenities, and at least two outputs.

Labor supply has a negative marginal utility, since it is a "bad." However, we assume that the manager is not a "workaholic," so

$$q_n$$

will never get so large as to threaten to bump up against a time constraint. This assumption allows us to avoid a more awkward form of the utility function without losing generality.

Constraints

The manager is also a consumer, and we include both the constraint faced by the individual as consumer and the constraints faced by the same individual as manager of the enterprise (all prices, vectors, and scalars are denoted p with appropriate subscript):

$$(2) \quad p_n q_n = p_c q_c$$

$$(3) \quad q_o = G(q_n, q_k)$$

$$(4) \quad r(q_f) = p_n q_n + p_k q_k + p_f q_f + p_a q_a$$

The first equation states that the individual's personal income

$$(p_n q_n)$$

equals personal consumption

$$(p_c q_c).$$

The second equation is the technological constraint

faced by the enterprise: outputs

$$q_o$$

are a (vector-valued) function G of the manager's own labor q_n and a vector q_k of all other inputs. (Note that amenities are not part of the production process.) G is assumed concave.

The third constraint is the budget constraint for the enterprise. "Fixed revenues" r are a concave function of the effort of the fundraiser hired by the manager to solicit contributions, manage endowment funds, submit proposals for grants, and negotiate contracts.

The other terms are self-explanatory: the entire equation states that fixed revenues equal total costs for all items including production inputs, fundraising, and managerial amenities. We do not here assume any "variable revenues."

The enterprise is assumed to be a price-taker in all markets. In the markets for

$$q_c, \quad q_k, \quad q_f, \text{ and } q_a,$$

the manager is in a perfectly-competitive market. For

$$p_n$$

we assume salary is set by custom or the board of trustees with an eye toward alternative employment open to the manager.

McGill and Wooten [1975, pp. 447-450] spoke of the presence of "conflicting standards of behavior," which could be interpreted as differing constraints. We have avoided here the problem of inconsistent constraints, but in a real-world case it may be possible that all the constraints cannot be met (or all the inequalities satisfied, if there are any) at once. Clarkson [1980] discusses types of constraints at some length.

Equilibrium

If we substitute (3) into (1), the resulting Lagrangean is:

$$(5) \quad L = U[q_c, q_n, q_a, G(q_n, q_k)]$$
$$+ \lambda_1[p_n q_n - p_c q_c]$$
$$+ \lambda_2[r(q_f - p_n q_n - p_k q_k - p_f q_f$$
$$- p_a q_a].$$

First-order conditions for maximization involve setting all first partial derivatives equal to zero. Second-order conditions are assumed satisfied from our concavity properties.

The first of the first-order conditions is:

$$(6) \quad \frac{\partial L}{\partial q_c} = \frac{\partial U}{\partial q_c} - 1 p_c = 0,$$

which states that the individual is an efficient consumer. Take any two consumption goods

$$q_{c1} \text{ and } q_{c2}:$$

$$\frac{\partial U}{\partial q_{c1}} = \lambda_1 p_{c1}, \quad \frac{\partial U}{\partial q_{c2}} = \lambda_1 p_{c2},$$

therefore,

$$\frac{\frac{\partial U}{\partial q_{c1}}}{\frac{\partial U}{\partial q_{c2}}} = \frac{p_{c1}}{p_{c2}},$$

which is the condition for efficient consumption. A similar argument applies to amenities:

$$(7) \quad \frac{\partial L}{\partial q_a} = \frac{\partial U}{\partial q_a} - \lambda_2 p_a = 0,$$

except that the Lagrange multiplier indicates that the purchases are made from the enterprise's budget, not out of the manager's personal income. This is not surprising since "nonpecuniary benefits" are an increasingly important part of compensation by all types of organizations.

The third equation is:

$$(8) \quad \frac{\partial L}{\partial q_k} = \frac{\partial U}{\partial G} \frac{\partial G}{\partial q_k} - \lambda_2 p_k = 0,$$

which for any two inputs

$$q_{k1} \text{ and } q_{k2}:$$

$$\frac{\dfrac{\partial G}{\partial q_{k1}}}{\dfrac{\partial G}{\partial q_{k2}}} = \frac{p_{k1}}{p_{k2}}$$

This is the condition for efficiency in input purchases; the enterprise is, with respect to any two
inputs other than the manager's time, operating on
its expansion path.

The next equation concerns fundraising:

$$(9) \quad \frac{\partial L}{\partial q_f} = \lambda_2 \frac{dr}{dq_f} - \lambda_2 p_f = 0,$$

which, in the same manner as the previous equation
for inputs, states that fundraising services will
be purchased efficiently by the charity manager.

Next is the equation for the manager's labor:

$$(10) \quad \frac{\partial L}{\partial q_n} = \frac{\partial U}{\partial q_n} + \frac{\partial U}{\partial G} \frac{\partial G}{\partial q_n} + \lambda_1 p_n - \lambda_2 p_n = 0$$

Rearranging terms we get:

$$\frac{\partial U}{\partial q_n} + \frac{\partial U}{\partial G} \frac{\partial G}{\partial q_n} = (\lambda_2 - \lambda_1) p_n$$

The left-hand side is the marginal disutility of
labor adjusted for the fact that the output of the
labor is valued by the manager; we may call the sum
of the terms the "net marginal disutility of labor."

Assume there are two different kinds of managerial labor, each of which has a different wage rate
attached. Then:

$$\frac{\dfrac{\partial U}{\partial q_{n1}} + \dfrac{\partial U}{\partial G}\dfrac{\partial G}{\partial q_{n1}}}{\dfrac{\partial U}{\partial q_{n2}} + \dfrac{\partial U}{\partial G}\dfrac{\partial G}{\partial q_{n2}}} = \frac{p_{n1}}{p_{n2}}$$

The manager's time is allocated efficiently between the two tasks.

The last two equations are the constraints:

(11) $\dfrac{\partial L}{\partial \lambda_1} = p_n q_n - p_c q_c = 0$

(12) $\dfrac{\partial L}{\partial \lambda_2} = r(q_f) - p_n q_n - p_k q_k - p_f q_f - p_a q_a = 0.$

It is clear that the private nonprofit enterprise is what we might call "piecewise efficient" in the input markets. For any two commodities of the same type, the enterprise (or manager as consumer) operates on its expansion path.

However, it is not clear what we can conclude about efficiency from examining the marginal rates of substitution for two different types of commodities. Between

$$q_c \text{ and } q_a$$

there is nothing but a tautology:

$$\frac{\dfrac{\partial U}{\partial q_c}}{\dfrac{\partial U}{\partial q_a}} = \frac{\lambda_1 p_c}{\lambda_2 p_a},$$

but the only way to evaluate

$$\lambda_1 \text{ and } \lambda_2$$

is to solve (6) and (7), or substitute for

$$\lambda_2$$

from (8). A similar problem holds for

$$q_c \text{ and } q_k,$$

91

which does not seem to be meaningful anyway. Equation (9), for

$$q_f,$$

cannot be paired with anything, but that makes sense since findraising is a separate activity from production.

Pairing labor with

$$q_c, \ q_a, \ \text{or} \ q_k$$

does not get us a clear solution either. Taking labor and another input for an example:

$$\frac{\frac{\partial U}{\partial q_n} + \frac{\partial U}{\partial G}\frac{\partial G}{\partial q_n}}{\frac{\partial U}{\partial G} \frac{\partial G}{\partial q_k}} \quad = \quad \frac{(\lambda_2 - \lambda_1)p_n}{\lambda_2 p_k}$$

$$= \quad (1 - \frac{\lambda_1}{\lambda_2} \frac{p_n}{p_k})$$

$$= \quad \frac{p_n}{p_k} (1 - \frac{\partial U/\partial q_c}{\partial U/\partial q_a}) \frac{p_a}{p_c},$$

which tells us nothing in particular about efficiency.

There is one success, however, taking an amenity and an input (one of the q_k variety):

$$\frac{\frac{\partial U}{\partial G} \frac{\partial G}{\partial q_k}}{\frac{\partial U}{\partial q_a}} = \frac{\lambda_2 p_k}{\lambda_2 p_a} .$$

When we cancel the

$$\lambda_2\text{'s}$$

we will show that the enterprise operates on the manager's expansion path, but not on the enterprise's one for production.

Extensions

The Manager's Own Labor

From (10) we know that the net marginal disutility of labor is proportional to its price:

$$\frac{\partial U}{\partial q_n} + \frac{\partial U}{\partial G} \frac{\partial G}{\partial q_n} = (\lambda_2 - \lambda_1) p_n$$

The two Lagrange multipliers on the right-hand side are respectively the marginal utility of the manager's own income

$$(\lambda_2)$$

and the marginal utility of the revenue generated for the enterprise

$$(\lambda_2).$$

Income is valued by the manager because of the consumption goods it buys. However, the manager also values the output of the firm; thus revenue to the enterprise is valued by the manager because of the output it can generate. Given a benevolent manager, it is not clear a priori which of

$$\lambda_1 \text{ and } \lambda_2$$

is greater.

Since

$$\frac{\partial U}{\partial G} \frac{\partial G}{\partial q_n}$$

is positive, then the net marginal disutility of labor associated with any particular quantity of labor is less than it otherwise would be. Therefore, the benevolent manager would work more than a selfish one. Nevertheless, how much the manager does work is dependent on the relation between

$$\lambda_1 \text{ and } \lambda_2,$$

93

that is, on how much the manager values own income versus enterprise revenue.

If

$$\lambda_2 = \lambda_1,$$

then the right-hand side of (10) is zero and the manager works until the marginal utility of output produced by labor equals the marginal disutility of labor. If

$$\lambda_2 > \lambda_1,$$

then the right-hand side of (10) is positive, and the marginal utility of the output produced by labor exceeds the marginal disutility of labor. The manager works more than in the preceding case.

If

$$\lambda_2 < \lambda_1,$$

then the right-hand side of (10) is negative, and the marginal utility of the output produced by labor falls short of the marginal disutility of labor. The manager works less than in the preceding two cases. Notice, however, this manager still works more than a selfish one.

A Special Case

Suppose that the manager's income is fixed and therefore unrelated to quantity of labor during the contract period. This "special" case is, of course, probably much more common than the more "general" one.

The problem then becomes:

(1) $\max U[q_c, q_n, q_a, q_o]$

(2)   s.t. $I = p_c q_c$

(3) $q_o = G(q_n, q_k)$

(4) $r(q_f) = I + p_k q_k + p_a q_a + p_f q_f$

Forming the Lagrangean:

(5) $L = U[q_c, q_n, q_a, G(q_n, q_k)] + \lambda_1[I - p_c q_c] + \lambda_2[r(q_f) - I - p_k q_k - p_a q_a - p_f q_f]$

First-order conditions then become:

(6) $\dfrac{\partial L}{\partial q_c} = \dfrac{\partial U}{\partial q_c} - \lambda_1 p_c = 0$

(7) $\dfrac{\partial L}{\partial q_a} = \dfrac{\partial U}{\partial q_a} - \lambda_2 p_a = 0$

(8) $\dfrac{\partial L}{\partial q_k} = \dfrac{\partial U}{\partial q_k} - \lambda_2 p_k = 0$

(9) $\dfrac{\partial L}{\partial q_f} = \lambda_2 \dfrac{dr}{dq_f} - \lambda_2 p_f = 0$

(10) $\dfrac{\partial L}{\partial q_n} = \dfrac{\partial U}{\partial q_n} + \dfrac{\partial U}{\partial G} \dfrac{\partial G}{\partial q_n} - \lambda_2 p_n = 0$

and the constraints again:

(11) $\dfrac{\partial L}{\partial \lambda_1} = I - p_c q_c = 0$

(12) $\dfrac{\partial L}{\partial \lambda_2} = r(q_f) - I - p_k q_k - p_a q_a - p_f q_f = 0$

If we assume that it is efficient to let the manager respond to the net marginal disutility of labor, then the enterprise operates on its expansion path with respect to any two quantities

$$q_k, \ q_n, \ \text{and} \ q_a.$$

(Consumption is included on the list if

$$\lambda_1 = \lambda_2.)$$

Fundraising of course is still purchased efficiently. Under this special case, then, parametric prices and managerial benevolence are sufficient to imply efficient production by a nonprofit enterprise.

The Bureau as a Nonprofit Enterprise

There is no reason to believe that the funds
for fixed revenues must come from more than one
source. If there is only one source of funds, then
the organization has already come close to being
a bureau of the funder no matter what the formal
arrangements are.

A bureau is simply an organization which is
part of another organization, and which therefore
finds that its revenue comes from a budget under
the control of the parent organization -- even if
the bureau itself sells some of its output at a positive price. Bureaus can be part of any other type
of organization: firm, government, or private nonprofit enterprise.

The important point about a bureau is that constraints on its budget can be set by someone outside
the organization. Even a "profit center" -- i.e.,
a bureau of a firm, in which the bureau's revenues
are obtained from sales in a market and which presumably exceed costs -- meets the two criteria for being
a bureau: no one in the bureau has a residual claim
on the profits, and someone outside the bureau can
set constraints on its budget. The difference between a bureau and another type of nonprofit enterprise is often one of degree: the bureau is responsible to a single parent organization, who may act
as donor, governing board, or client, or a combination of these. In an independent nonprofit organization, these roles are spread among several individuals and groups.

The significance of

$$q_f$$

in a theory of the bureau is that it can be interpreted to include testifying before Congress on the
forthcoming budget, making a presentation to the
board of directors about the expansion of a new division, or campaigning before the dean on behalf of
a faculty member up for tenure at a private university.

Of course the parent organization will probably
set other constraints on the bureau besides those
placed on its revenues. These would have to be

incorporated into any model of a particular bureau
or type of bureau. We could expect them to differ,
for example, with the type of parent organization.
However, the idea behind

$$q_f$$

should be kept in mind for other constraints as well:
just because an item is "fixed" from one point of
view does not mean that someone in the bureau cannot
find a way to "stretch" the constraint a little bit
or work to get it shifted out.

In short, the model of the private nonprofit
enterprise that has been proposed in this chapter
is quite general. It is a first cousin of the
managerial-discretion model of the firm and can be
applied to the bureau. Perhaps this is the beginning
of a contribution to a more specified neoclassical
theory of organization.

Conclusion

In answer to the question: "Does the private
nonprofit enterprise purchase its inputs efficiently?"
we give a qualified "yes": the manager's concern
for the output of the enterprise leads the enterprise
to operate along its expansion path, at least for
some pairs of inputs. Under circumstances common
to most enterprises (our "special case"), the enterprise operates on its expansion path everywhere.
Thus, if a nonprofit enterprise purchases its inputs
inefficiently, that is not necessarily because it
is nonprofit. Whether from the desire for prestige
or from a benevolent desire to serve society well,
the manager interested in the enterprise's output
will try to purchase inputs in an efficient combination in the piecewise manner described above.

What then impedes the manager from making the
efficient choice? If it can indeed be demonstrated
that private nonprofit enterprises operate more inefficiently than do firms at their chosen level of
output, the answer must lie somewhere other than
in the nonprofit characteristic <u>per</u> <u>se</u>. Several
alternatives have been suggested. First, managerial
skill may be less in the nonprofit sector. The first
textbook in management of nonprofit enterprises was
not published until 1975 [Anthony, 1980, p. 7].

Second, the output(s) of the enterprise may be difficult to measure, much less evaluate. Third, monitoring costs and procedures may differ from those used in firms [Clarkson, 1980, p. 21].

All of these characteristics are likely to change over time as we begin to know more about how nonprofit enterprises fit into the economic system. However, none of them implies that nonprofitness itself is a cause of inefficiency in the use of resources.

CHAPTER V

SUMMARY AND CONCLUSION

Summary

At the beginning of Chapter I we asked five questions about nonprofit enterprises: "What are they?," "What do they do?," "Why are they created?," "How do they operate?," and "How well do they perform?" In the pages and chapters that followed we considered how far traditional neoclassical economic theory has gone and can go in answering these questions, and how well we can apply these answers to describe nonprofit organizations in the real world, specifically research libraries or art museums.

Economists generally have begun to agree on the answer to the first question. The ownership definition seems the most general and useful one: a nonprofit enterprise is an organization none of whose members has a property right over any fraction of the difference between its revenues and costs. Thus neoclassical economists have established a common starting point for the subject.

The question of what nonprofit enterprises do is central to the broad issue of how far neoclassical methods can go in describing and evaluating their activities. Musgrave's taxonomy of "fiscal functions" (allocation, distribution, and stabilization), clearly inspired by neoclassical categories, can be used as the basis for a more comprehensive classification of the economic functions of nonprofit organizations.

The contribution of Chapter II is to add two functions to the list and specify more clearly both the role that nonprofit enterprises play in the economy and the scope and limits of neoclassical methods of characterizing and evaluating that role. The complete list of the five economic functions of public and private nonprofit enterprise, and the major types of activities undertaken to carry out those functions reads as follows:

1. Environmental

   a. Taste formation
   b. Autonomous change in technology
   c. Determination of resource endowment

2. Systemic

   a. Ownership determination
   b. Trust establishment

      (i) Economic socialization
      (ii) Contract enforcement

   c. Provision and facilitation of market
      information

3. Allocative

   a. Allocation of public goods and goods
      with external costs and benefits
   b. Promotion of competition
   c. Encouragement of merit goods and
      discouragement of demerit goods
   d. Reduction of risk and use of social
      rather than private discount rates

4. Distributive: redistribution in cash or
   in kind

5. Stabilizational: promotion of full employment, price stability, external
   balance, and stable growth

The first two functions establish the circumstances
for market success; the last three correct for market
failures. (Compare this list with the list of neoclassical assumptions in Chapter I.) Traditional
neoclassical welfare economics assumes that all these
activities have been (or will be) performed outside
the market system if the economy is to allocate resources efficiently. Therefore, according to the
logic of neoclassical theory, the efficiency of a
market economy depends partly on the activities of
its nonmarket sectors. In addition, the same theory
assumes away goals other than allocative efficiency
and stable growth; an economy whose members care
about other goals (such as freedom, cooperation,
or cultural values) must rely partly on its nonmarket
sectors to achieve them.

The third and fourth questions are about the motives behind the individuals who create nonprofit organizations and the constraints they face in doing so. The lessons of Chapter III are that both differ with the type of organization involved -- in particular, both differ between nonprofit enterprises and firms.

Selfish motives toward private goods can explain the creation of markets for exchange transactions between individuals and firms. Those same motives and the existence of public goods and other free-rider problems can explain the creation of governments, including municipalities, special districts, and independent authorities. Why then, in an economy of selfish individuals, would there be any motive to create private nonprofit enterprises? The answer is that there would be no such motive for many private nonprofit enterprises (and some activities of governments, e.g., encouragement of merit goods).

The motives for creation of private nonprofit enterprises must come from the desire to perform the five economic functions. Selfishness suffices as an explanation for why someone would create an organization to perform them but not as an explanation for why that organization would be private and nonprofit. Why would a selfish person do something if not for profit or the desire to avoid free-rider problems? The motive for creation of private nonprofit enterprise must come at least partly from nonselfish motives.

Many of the constraints under which nonprofit enterprises operate also differ from those which apply to firms. The no-profit constraint itself is the basic distinction between the two types of organization, but many other types of constraints can be explained as attempts by society, or by the organization itself, to enforce certain types of behavior on its employees, particularly behavior related to keeping selfish motives in check.

The last question on our list is: "How well do nonprofit enterprises perform?" Chapter IV argues that even though it is not yet possible to evaluate the question of whether the outputs of nonprofit enterprises are in the right mix at the right levels, we can by neoclassical methods provide a partial answer to another important question: "Does a nonprofit enterprise purchase inputs in efficient combinations?" The answer is a qualified "yes": as long as the manager is concerned with the output of the enterprise, it will be at least "piecewise efficient" with respect to pairs of inputs of the same type (e.g., two types of capital), the enterprise will operate on its expansion path, i.e., efficiently. In an important and common "special case" it will be completely efficient. Thus for possible sources of inefficiency in nonprofit enterprises we should look not at the nonprofit constraint but at measurability of output, internal organizational constraints, and elsewhere.

This study has thus made three contributions to the development of an economics of nonprofit enterprise. First, it has pointed out the limits of neoclassical economic theory in guiding us toward normative judgments about their performance and provided a characterization of the roles played by nonprofit enterprises in the economic system. Second, it has provided a rationale for the existence of private nonprofit enterprises along with firms and governments in an economy of neoclassically rational individuals. Third, it has demonstrated the efficiency of nonprofit enterprise in the purchase of inputs. In some cases we may have provided answers; in others we have at least carried out the important task or organizing the questions.

Further Research

The economics of nonprofit organizations has been a growing field in recent years, as have been other areas related to it (health economics, for example). It is still, however, more of a collection of disparate innovations than a unified theory. Further research should proceed along three lines: the relation of the organization to its members, the relation of the organization to its donors and clientele, and the relation of the organization to the economic system.

The study of the relation of the firm to its employees is what Leibenstein refers to as "micro-microeconomics" [1979, p. 477]. Though a literature on this has existed since Adam Smith's day, neoclassical theory has until recently done scarcely more than assume such problems away. The present study

102

is no exception; Chapter IV, for example, is what Leibenstein would describe as a "complex-objective-function" approach [p. 478]. The group-choice problems within the organization which are ignored in that chapter are part of the "micro-micro" approach. What is needed is an expansion of this approach through the acknowledgement that organizations are simply networks of more or less routinized transaction among individuals, and the development of ways to infer the behavior of the organization from the decisions made by its members. This has already been done to some extent for firms [e.g., Williamson, 1967, Chapter 8] and governments [Mueller, 1976, 1979], but they should also be studied for nonprofit enterprises.

Other tasks to be performed under this heading include a specification of the constraints under which nonprofit enterprises operate and the policy implications of different types of regulatory constraints. Which constraints, for example, act to encourage self-centered behavior by the manager, and which to discourage it? In addition, a theory of the bureau could perhaps be devised as a special case of the nonprofit enterprise, in which specific constraints on behavior are set by the parent organization.

The second line of research concerns the relation between the nonprofit enterprise and its donors and clientele. These relationships should be seen as the nonmarket analog to the market process in the ordinary economics of exchange. Here, however, information problems are important in a model of donation and fundraising; a "lemon" may be more difficult to detect if it is a college or relief agency than if it is an automobile [Boulding, 1973]. A theory of clientele is necessary for those nonprofit enterprises that produce quasi-public goods (e.g., education) rather than pure public goods (e.g., defense). There has been some work done in this area already [Rose-Ackerman, 1980].

The next step in the economics of nonprofit enterprise would be to develop a general equilibrium (and disequilibrium) model that incudes the determination of the optimum level of output of nonprofit enterprises. Such a model would have to endogenize taste, technology, etc. -- even property rights [Boulding, 1977; Conn, 1978].

It may be expecting too much of neoclassical theory to believe it can incorporate such variables as "trust" and "merit goods." However, this is precisely the point: those who attempt to apply a neoclassical mentality to the study of nonprofit enterprises are applying a theory that is too narrow for the phenomena being studied. Therefore the conclusions that come up are likely to be distorted or just plain wrong. Until we have completed the extension of neoclassical theory or supplemented it with something else, we must be circumspect in our claims about the economics of nonprofit enterprise.

Research on measurement problems should continue along with that on theoretical ones. Both conceptualization of new performance measures and basic data gathering are needed. This is true not only in industries where work has already been done, such as education or health, but in others covered less well, such as libraries, the arts, and religion.

Conclusion

It is clear that the emerging field of the economics of nonprofit enterprises can draw from many different existing fields and traditions in economics: comparative economic systems, industrial organization, public finance, etc. Like other branches of economics, it should draw on outside fields as well: general systems theory, social psychology, organizational behavior, etc. It will probably find its niche somewhere in the category of grants economics, social economics, and hopefully, "normative science."

What are the long-run implications of the opening up of this field? At the present time, public and private nonprofit enterprises seem to be coming under a deep philosophical attack. The careful study of their relationship to the economy can perhaps shed light on the question of whether nonprofit enterprises are frills, distractions, wasteful and misguided aberrations, or whether they are the foundations on which a mixed economy rests.

Bibliography

Alchian, Armen and Allen, William R. Exchange and Production: Competition, Coordination, and Control. Second edition. Belmont, California: Wadsworth, 1977.

American Historical Association. Annual Report.

Ames, Edward. Soviet Economic Processes. Homewood, Illinois: Irwin, 1965.

Anthony, Robert N. and Hirzlinger, Regina E. Management Control in Nonprofit Organizations. Homewood, Illinois: Irwin, 1980.

Arrow, Kenneth J. "A Difficulty in the Concept of Social Welfare," Journal of Political Economy, August 1950, 58(4), pp. 328-346.

_____. "Economic Welfare and the Allocation of Resources for Invention," in The Rate and Duration of Inventive Activity: Economic and Social Factors. Princeton: Princeton University Press for the National Bureau of Economic Research, 1962, pp. 609-626. Reprinted in Lamberton, 1971, pp. 141-159.

_____. "Gifts and Exchanges." Philosophy and Public Affairs, Summer 1974, 1(4), pp. 343-362. Reprinted in Phelps [1975], pp. 13-28.

_____. The Limits of Organization. New York: Norton, 1974.

_____. and Hahn, F.H. General Competitive Analysis. Amsterdam: North-Holland, 1971.

_____. Social Choice and Individual Values. Revised edition. New York: Wiley, 1963.

Asimov, Isaac. Foundation, New York: Avon, 1951.

_____. Foundation and Empire, New York: Avon, 1952.

_____. Second Foundation, New York: Avon, 1953.

Association for the Study of Grants Economy. Tenth

Anniversary Brochure, 1968-1978, Haldenweg, Germany: Center for the Study of the Grants Economy, 1978.

Atkinson, Anthony B. and Stiglitz, Joseph E. Lectures on Public Economics. New York: McGraw-Hill, 1980.

Atkinson, Richard C. "Federal Support in the Social Sciences," Science, 22 February 1980, 207 (4433), p. 829.

Barash, David P. Sociobiology and Behavior. New York: Elsevier, 1977.

Bator, Francis M. "The Simple Analytics of Welfare Maximization." American Economic Review, March 1957, 47(1), pp. 22-59. Reprinted in Breit [1971], pp. 455-483.

_____. "The Anatomy of Market Failure." Quarterly Journal of Economics, August 1958, 72(1), pp. 351-379. Reprinted in Breit [1971], pp. 518-537, and Mansfield [1979], pp. 425-450.

_____. Economic Theory and Operations Analysis. Fourth edition. Englewood Cliffs, New Jersey: Prentice-Hall, 1977.

Becker, Gary. "Altruism, Egoism, and Genetic Fitness: Economics and Sociobiology." Journal of Economic Literature, September 1976, 14(3), pp. 817-826. Reprinted as Chapter 13 of Becker [1976].

Bergson, Abram. "A Reformulation of Certain Aspects of Welfare Economics." Quarterly Journal of Economics, February 1938, 52(1), pp. 310-334.

Berle, Adolf A. and Means, Gardiner C. The Modern Corporation and Private Property. Revised edition. New York: Harcourt, Brace, and World, 1968.

Boulding, Kenneth E. A Reconstruction of Economics. New York: Wiley, 1950.

_____. "Welfare Economics." A Survey of Contemporary Economics, Vol. II, edited by Bernard F. Haley. Homewood, Illinois: Irwin for the

American Economic Association, 1952, pp. 1-34.

_____. The Image: Knowledge in Life and Society. Ann Arbor, Michigan: Univeristy of Michigan Press, 1956.

_____. "General Systems Theory -- The Skeleton of Science." Management Science, April 1956, 2(3), pp. 197-208. Reprinted in Buckley [1968], pp. 3-10.

_____. Economics as a Science. New York: McGraw-Hill, 1970.

_____. "Fun and Games with the Gross National Product: The Role of Misleading Indicators in Social Policy," in Harold W. Helfrich, Jr., ed., The Environmental Crisis. New Haven, Connecticut: Yale University Press, 1970, pp. 157-170. Reprinted in Kenneth E. Boulding, Collected Papers. Volume Three: Political Economy. Larry D. Singell, ed. Boulder, Colorado: Colorado Associated Universities Press, 1973, pp. 467-482.

_____. "Towards a Pure Theory of Foundations." Non-Profit Report, March 1972, 5(3) Supplement.

_____. "Toward the Development of a Cultural Economics." Social Science Quarterly, September 1972, 53(2), pp. 267-284.

_____. "Intersects: The Peculiar Organizations." Chapter 6 of Challenge to Leadership: Managing in a Changing World. New York: Free Press for the Conference Board, 1973, pp. 179-201.

_____. "Notes on Goods, Services, and Cultural Economics." Journal of Cultural Economics, 1(1), Spring 1977, pp. 1-14.

_____. "A Program for Research in Human Betterment." Unpublished, 1977.

_____. Ecodynamics: A New Theory of Societal Evolution. Beverly Hills, California: Sage, 1978.

Branson, William H. Macroeconomic Theory and Policy.

New York: Harper and Row, 1972.

Breit, William and Hochman, Harold M. Readings in Microeconomics. Second edition. New York: Holt, Reinhart and Winston, 1971.

Brown, Maryann Kevin. "Library Data, Statistics, and Information: Progress Toward Comparability." Special Libraries, November 1980, 71(11), pp. 475-484.

Buchanan, James M. "An Economic Theory of Clubs." Economica, February 1965, 32(125), pp. 1-4. Reprinted in Breit [1971], pp. 547-556.

Buckley, Walter, ed. Modern Systems Research for the Behavioral Scientist. Chicago: Aldine, 1968.

Cheung, Steven N.S. The Theory of Share Tenancy, with Special Application to Asian Agriculture and the First Phase of Taiwan Land Reform. Chicago: University of Chicago Press, 1969.

Chiang, Alpha C. Fundamental Methods of Mathematical Economics. New York: McGraw-Hill, 1967.

Clarkson, Kenneth, and Donald L. Martin, eds. The Economics of Nonproprietory Organizations. Greenwich, Connecticut: JAI Press, 1980.

Collard, David. Altruism and Economy: A Study of Non-Selfish Economics. New York: Oxford University Press, 1978.

Commons, John R. Institutional Economics: Its Place in Political Economy. New York: Macmillan, 1934.

Conn, David. "Economic Theory and Comparative Economic Systems: A Partial Literature Survey." Journal of Comparative Economics, December 1978, 2(4), pp. 355-381.

Cyert, Richard M. and March, James G. A Behavioral Theory of the Firm. Englewood Cliffs, New Jersey: Prentice-Hall, 1963.

Dewey, Donald. Microeconomics: The Analysis of Prices and Markets. New York: Oxford University Press, 1975.

Dickinson, F.G., ed. <u>Philanthrophy and Public Policy</u>. New York: National Bureau of Economic Research, 1962.

Dowling, William F. "Consensus Management at Graphic Controls," <u>Organizational Dynamics</u>, Winter 1977, pp. 23-47.

Dye, Richard Forsythe. "Personal Charitable Contributions: Tax Effects and Other Motives." Unpublished Ph.D. dissertation, University of Michigan, 1976.

<u>The Economics of Charity: Essays on the Comparative Economics and Ethics of Giving and Selling, with Applications to Blood</u>. London: Institute of Economics Research, 1962.

Edgeworth, Francis Ysidro. <u>Mathematical Phychics: An Essay on the Application of Mathematics to the Moral Sciences</u>. London: Kegan Paul, 1881. Reprint: New York: Augustus M. Kelley, 1967.

Etzioni, Amitai, and Doty, Pamela. "Profit in Not-for-Profit Corporations: The Example of Health Care." <u>Political Science Quarterly</u>, Fall 1976, 91(3), pp. 433-453.

Frey, Bruno S. <u>Modern Political Economy</u>. New York: Wiley, 1978.

_____ and Pommerehne, Werner W. <u>An Economic Analysis of the Museum</u>. Zurich: Institute for Empirical Research in Economics, University of Zurich, August 1979. (<u>Discussion Paper</u> 7906.)

Friedman, Milton. <u>Price Theory: A Provisional Text</u>. Revised edition. Chicago: Aldine, 1962.

_____. "The Social Responsibility of Business is to Increase Its Profits." <u>The New York Times Magazine</u>, September 13, 1970. Abridged in Kenneth G. Elzinga, ed., <u>Economics: A Reader</u>. New York: Harper and Row, 1978, pp. 52-55.

Furubotn, Eirik and Pejovich, Svetozar, eds., <u>The Economics of Property Rights</u>. Cambridge, Massachusetts: Ballinger, 1974.

Garvin, David A. The Economics of University Behavior. New York: Academic Press, 1980.

Gassler, Robert Scott. "The Economics of Nonprofit Enterprise: Suggestions for an Extension of Microeconomic Theory." Forum for Social Economics, Summer, 1979, pp. 18-23.

_____. "The Economics of Nonprofit Enterprise: An Extension of Microeconomic Theory." Presented at the annual meeting of the Association for Comparative Economic Studies, Atlanta, Georgia, December 1979.

Ginzberg, Eli; Hiestand, Dale L.; and Reubens, Beatrice G. The Pluralistic Economy. New York: McGraw-Hill, 1965.

Graaff, J. de V. Theoretical Welfare Economics. Cambridge: Cambridge University Press, 1957.

Gross, Malvern J., Jr. and Warshauer, William, Jr. Financial and Accounting Guide for Nonprofit Organizations. Third edition. New York: Wiley, 1979.

Hansmann, Henry. "The Role of Nonprofit Enterprise." Yale Law Journal, April 1980, 89(5), pp. 835-901.

Heertje, Arnold. Economics and Technical Change. London: Weidenfield and Nicholson, 1973.

Henderson, James M. and Quandt, Richard E. Microeconomic Theory: A Mathematical Approach. Third edition. New York: McGraw-Hill, 1980.

Hicks, J.R. Value and Capital: An Inquiry into Some Fundamental Principles of Economic Theory. Second edition. New York: Oxford University Press, 1946.

Hirshleifer, Jack. Price Theory and Applications. Second edition. Englewood Cliffs, New Jersey: Prentice-Hall, 1980.

Hochman, Harold M. and Rodgers, James D. "Pareto Optimal Redistribution." American Economic

<u>Review</u>, September 1969, 59(4), pp. 542-557.

_____ and _____. "Pareto Optimal Redistribution: Reply." <u>American Economic Review</u>,
December 1980, pp. 997-1002.

Horvath, Janos. "On a Positive Theory of the Voluntary Nonprofit Sector: a Grants Economy Approach." Unpublished draft prepared for AEA
annual meeting, 1978.

Intriligator, Michael D. <u>Mathematical Optimization
and Economic Theory</u>. Englewood Cliffs, New
Jersey: Prentice-Hall, 1971.

James, Estelle. "A Contribution to the Theory of
the Non-Profit Organization." Unpublished,
n.d.

Joseph, Hyman. "On Economic Theories of Hospital
Behavior." <u>Journal of Economics and Business</u>,
Fall 1974, 27(1), pp. 69-74.

Judge, Anthony. "Wanted: New Types of Social Entity; Part 2: Matrix Organization and Organizational Networks." <u>International Associations</u>,
1971, (3), pp. 154-170.

Keating, Barry P. and Keating, Maryann O. <u>Not-for-
Profit</u>. Glenn Ridge, New Jersey: Thomas Horton
and Daughters, 1980.

Kirschen, E.S., <u>et al</u>. Economic Policy in Our Time,
Vol. 1: <u>General Theory</u>. Chicago: Rand-
McNally, 1964.

Knight, Frank H. <u>Risks, Uncertainty, and Profit</u>.
New York: Harper, 1921.

_____. "Social Economic Organization." <u>The
Economic Organization</u>. New York: Harper &
Row, 1951, pp. 3-30. Reprinted in Breit, 1971,
pp. 3-19.

Koopmans, Tjalling C. <u>Three Essays on the State
of Economic Science</u>. New York: McGraw-Hill,
1957.

Kurz, Mordecai. "Altruism as an Outcome of Social
Interaction." <u>American Economic Review</u>, May

1978, 68(2), pp. 216-222.

_____. "Altruistic Equilibrium." In _Economic Progress, Private Values, and Public Policy: Essays in Honor of William Fellner_, edited by Bela Balassa and Richard Nelson. Amsterdam: Elsevier, 1977.

Lamberton, D.M., ed., _Economics of Information and Knowledge: Selected Readings_. Baltimore: Penguin Books, 1971.

Leibenstein, Harvey. "Allocative Efficiency vs. 'X-Efficiency'." _American Economic Review_, June 1966, 56(3), pp. 392-415.

_____. _Beyond Economic Man: A New Foundation for Microeconomics_. Cambridge: Harvard University Press, 1980.

_____. "A Branch of Economics is Missing: Micro-Micro Theory," _Journal of Economic Literature_, June 1979, 17(2), pp. 477-502.

Lindsay, Cotton M. "A Theory of Government Enterprise," _Journal of Political Economy_, October 1976, 84(5), pp. 1061-1078.

Lipsey, Richard G., and Steiner, Peter O. _Economics_. Sixth edition. New York: Harper and Row, 1981.

Malenbaum, Helen. "Review of Steven N.S. Cheung, _Theory of Share Tenancy_." _Journal of Economic History_, December 1970, 30(4), pp. 875-879.

Mansfield, Edwin, ed., _Microeconomics: Selected Readings_. Third edition. New York: Norton, 1979.

Marris, Robin. "A Model of the Managerial Enterprise." _Quarterly Journal of Economics_, May 1963, 77(2), pp. 185-209.

_____. _The Economic Theory of "Managerial Capitalism_. New York: Macmillan, 1964.

McCain, Roger A. "Reflections on the Cultivation of Taste." _Journal of Cultural Economics_, June 1979, 3(9), pp. 30-53.

McGill, Michael E. and Wooten, Leland M. "Management in the Third Sector." _Public Administration Review_, September/October 1975, 35(5), pp. 444-445.

McGill, William J. "Memorandum to Columbia University Students Re Facts on University Investments," May 3, 1978.

Meyer, Robert A. _Microeconomic Decisions_. Boston: Houghton Mifflin, 1976.

Migue, Jean-Luc and Belanger, Gerard. "Toward a General Theory of Managerial Discretion." _Public Choice_, Spring 1974, 17, pp. 27-47.

Montias, J. Michael. _The Structure of Economic Systems_. New Haven: Yale University Press, 1976.

Mueller, Dennis C. "Public Choice: A Survey." _Journal of Economic Literature_, June 1976, 14 (2), pp. 395-433.

_____. _Public Choice_. New York: Cambridge University Press, 1979.

Musgrave, Richard A. _The Theory of Public Finance: A Study in Public Economy_. New York: McGraw-Hill, 1959.

_____ and Musgrave, Peggy B. _Public Finance in Theory and Practice_. Third edition. New York: McGraw-Hill, 1980.

Neuberger, Egon and Duffy, William J. _Comparative Economic Systems, a Decision-Making Approach_. Boston: Allyn and Bacon, 1976.

Newhouse, Joseph P. "Toward a Theory of Nonprofit Institutions: An Economic Model of a Hospital." _American Economic Review_, March 1979, 60(1), pp. 64-75.

Nicholson, Walter. _Microeconomic Theory: Basic Principles and Extensions_. Second edition. Hinsdale, Illinois: Dryden Press, 1978.

Niskanen, William A. _Bureaucracy and Representative Government_, Chicago: Aldine Atherton, 1971.

Oleck, Howard L. <u>Non-Profit Corporations, Organiza-tions, and Associations</u>. Third edition. Engle-wood Cliffs, New Jersey: Prentice-Hall, 1974.

Pei, Mario. <u>The Story of Language</u>. Revised edition. New York: New American Library, 1965.

Phelps, Edmund S. <u>Altruism, Morality, and Economic Theory</u>. New York: Russell Sage Foundation, 1975.

Quirk, James and Saposnik, Rubin. <u>Introduction to General Equilibrium Theory and Welfare Econom-ics</u>. New York: McGraw-Hill, 1974.

Rose-Ackerman, Susan. "The Charity Market: Paying Customers and Quality Control." New Haven, Connecticut: Yale University Institution for Social and Policy Studies, June 1980. (PONPO No. 19)

Samuelson, Paul Anthony. <u>Foundations of Economic Analysis</u>. New York: Atheneum, 1979.

_____. "The Economic Role of Private Activity," in <u>A Dialogue on the Proper Economic Role of the State</u>. Chicago: University of Chicago Graduate School of Business, 1963. (Selected Papers No. 7, The Graduate School of Business). Reprinted as Chapter 9 of <u>Economics: Readings, Issues, and Cases</u>, edited by Edwin Mansfield. Third edition. New York: Norton, 1980.

Schelling, Thomas C. "Altruism, Meanness, and Other Potentially Strategic Behaviors." <u>American Economic Review</u>, May 1978, 68(2), pp. 229-230.

Scherer, F.M. <u>Industrial Market Structure and Econom-ic Performance</u>. Second edition. Chicago: Rand McNally, 1980.

<u>Scholarly Communication: The Report of the National Enquiry</u>. Baltimore: John Hopkins University Press, 1979.

Shepherd, William G. <u>The Economics of Industrial Organization</u>. Englewood Cliffs, New Jersey: Prentice-Hall, 1979.

Simon, Herbert A. <u>Administrative Behavior</u>. Third

edition. New York: Free Press, 1976.

_____. "Rational Decision Making in Business Organizations." <u>American Economic Review</u>, September 1979, 69(4), pp. 493-513.

Stigler, George J. "The Economics of Information." <u>Journal of Political Economy</u>, June 1961, 69(3), pp. 213-225. Reprinted in Lamberton, 1971, pp. 61-82.

Titmus, Richard M. <u>The Gift Relationship: From Human Blood to Social Policy</u>. New York: Random House, 1971.

Turner, Jonathan H. <u>The Structure of Sociological Theory</u>. Homewood, Illinois: Dorsey, 1974.

Turvey, Ralph. <u>Economic Analysis and Public Enterprises</u>. London: George Allen and Unwin, 1971.

U.S. Office of the Federal Register. <u>United States Government Manual</u>, 1979-1980. Washington, D.C.: U.S. Government Printing Office, 1979.

Varian, Hal R. <u>Microeconomic Analysis</u>. New York: Norton, 1978.

Weisbrod, Burton Allen. <u>The Voluntary Nonprofit Sector: An Economic Analysis</u>. Lexington, Massachusetts: Lexington Books, 1977.

_____. "The Private Nonprofit Sector: Facts in Search of a Theory, or Toward a Field of Institutionalmetrics." University of Wisconsin Institute of Research on Poverty, Discussion Paper No. 501-78, July 1978.

Williamson, Oliver E. <u>The Economics of Discretionary Behavior: Managerial Objectives in a Theory of the Firm</u>. Chicago: Markham, 1967.

Wonnacott, Paul and Wonnacott, Ronald. <u>An Introduction to Microeconomics</u>. New York: McGraw-Hill, 1979.

Young, Dennis R. <u>If Not for Profit, For What? A Behavioral Theory of the Nonprofit Sector Based on Entrepreneurship</u>. Lexington, Massachusetts: Lexington Books, 1983.

Index

About the Author

Robert Scott Gassler is Assistant Professor of Economics at Guilford College in Greensboro, North Carolina. He earned his AB in economics from Oberlin, an MS from the Columbia University School of Library Service, an MA in economics from the University of Washington (Seattle), and his Ph.D. in economics from the University of Colorado. This book is a revision of his dissertation, written under Kenneth Boulding.

Dr. Gassler has published in both economics and library science. His interests include comparative economic systems, public sector economics, the economics of the library industry, peace studies, and the interaction of economic, political, and social institutions.

Dr. Gassler is a member of a number of organizations, including the American Economic Association, the American Library Association, the Association for Social Economics, and the Society for General Systems Research. He is active in the Unitarian Church of Greensboro.